Strengthening the Adult Sunday School Class

Strengthening the Adult Sunday School Class

Dick Murray

Creative Leadership Series
Lyle E. Schaller, Editor

Abingdon Press / Nashville

STRENGTHENING
THE ADULT SUNDAY SCHOOL CLASS

Library of Congress Cataloging in Publication Data
MURRAY, DICK, 1924—
    Strengthening the adult Sunday school class.
    (Creative leadership series)
    Bibliography: p.
    1. Christian education of adults.   2. Sunday-schools.
    I. Title.   II. Series.
    BV1488.M87   268'.434   81-3667   AACR2

ISBN 0-687-39989-0 (pbk.)

MANUFACTURED BY THE PARTHENON PRESS AT
NASHVILLE, TENNESSEE, UNITED STATES OF AMERICA

To M. Leo Rippy, Sr.
Pioneer Adult Educator and Mentor to many

and to Joyce Martin Murray
my wife and friend

Foreword

"Our adult Sunday school classes used to be the backbone of this church, but now our older classes are beginning to fade away and we haven't been able to get any new ones started. What do you think we should do?"

"The couples class my wife and I helped start back in 1948 probably meant more to us than anything else we've been involved in, outside our family, in all the years we've been married. Our oldest son and his wife now go to a church where they don't have that kind of adult class. We believe they're missing a lot. Have adult classes simply gone out of style or is there any advice we can offer them to help get an adult class started in their church?"

"In the old days the adult classes provided a supply of teachers for children and youth. Now our adult classes have shrunk to only two and we can't get teachers without disrupting those two classes. What are we going to do?"

"Our new Sunday school class for young adults now has

close to eighty enrolled in it, and we usually have between fifty and sixty there on a typical Sunday. Don't you think that's too large? Wouldn't it be better if we divided this class in two smaller classes?"

These are representative of the scores of questions being asked by both pastors and laypersons about the adult Sunday school. For at least a century the adult Sunday school was the backbone, the center of strength, and the most vital program in tens of thousands of Protestant churches across the United States and Canada. In many congregations that statement still can be made in the present tense, but in others it has to be in the past tense.

A variety of diagnostic statements have been made about the reasons for that decline. These range from the urbanization of society to the increase in the number of wives employed outside the home, to the impact of television in increasing competition for people's time on the weekends, to the failure of the seminaries to train future pastors in the care and feeding of adult classes, to the increased mobility of the population.

In this pioneering book, Dick Murray breaks new ground both in the diagnosis of the reasons for this decline and in offering a comprehensive prescription for the revitalization of the adult Sunday school. The reader who is looking for a "cookbook" that will give precise instructions on how to start a new class will find it here. The person who seeks to understand the hidden dynamics of that closely knit, cohesive, and caring adult fellowship will find the answers in Professor Murray's analysis. The superintendent who has difficulty in finding effective teachers for adult classes will be rewarded by a series of specific suggestions on the identification, recruitment, training, and support of adult teachers. The minister in the small church will find that the Reverend Murray understands his type of congregation and offers several useful ideas for enriching the Sunday school in the small membership congregation. The active leaders of thousands of big, established adult classes will find great satisfaction in discovering that much of what they have done intuitively and informally is critical to the effectiveness of these classes.

Perhaps the most important single contribution of this book, however, is the strong affirmation of the role of the adult Sunday school class as a channel for God's grace in helping the individual adult on his or her personal and religious pilgrimage. Through the fellowship, the caring for one another, the reflecting on the lessons, the working together on the class project, the social activities, and the inspiration of the Scriptures, the members of the adult class gain both the opportunity to learn about the Christian faith and also many opportunities to practice the teaching of our Lord. In other words, the adult class has a very important place in the church in the 1980s and 1990s!

This volume is one in a series of books directed at the creative leaders of congregations. This series was developed as a means of providing help to leaders who seek creative new ideas on pressing congregational concerns. Professor Murray's contribution to this series discusses one of the most important issues facing the Protestant churches today. We are grateful for his positive, lucid, and readable analysis of the myths and realities of adult classes.

Lyle E. Schaller
Yokefellow Institute
Richmond, Indiana

Contents

Preface

I was "born" into the Brownie Class of First United Methodist Church, Des Moines, Iowa. My newly married parents joined the class the year before, in 1923, and my birth was one of several to members of the class the next year.

Started in 1921 by six couples, the class was named after its first teacher, Mr. Ed Brown, and the birth of this Young Couples' Class was part of a wave of such classes across the country in the years following World War I. Up until that time most adult Sunday school classes were divided by sex, with many strong women's classes and men's classes.

As I grew up, I was quite conscious of the importance of the Brownie Class to my parents. They weathered the depression of the thirties, the raising of me and my three brothers, and the normal trials and tribulations of married life, within the warmth of that class. In 1960 my mother died, after a long illness, and the class both sustained her as she struggled with her illness and death and was of crucial importance to my father as he recovered from nursing her and prepared for his retirement a few years later.

In 1973 the Brownie Class decided to stop meeting on Sunday mornings as a class (the class was fifty-two years old), and to give up its room to another class which needed it. The class has continued to have regular social meetings, with nearly all of its living members well into their eighties.

My lifelong association with *this* adult Sunday school class, and my awareness of its crucial role in the life of my parents, formed the background of my interest in adult Sunday school classes and my search for their particular geniuses.

As a pastor in Texas and New York, a National Missionary in Kentucky, and a staff member of a large church in Tennessee, I had the opportunity to observe a wide variety of adult classes over several years. In 1955 I became director of adult work of the Board of Education of the Texas Annual Conference, and for the next five years worked in many churches in East Texas and in the Houston area, helping solve adult class problems and training teachers of adults.

Many of my views of adult church education have changed radically over the years. My understanding of and appreciation for the ongoing adult Sunday school class has grown a great deal: in fact, from mild scorn to warm understanding. This has been tied to a changing understanding of how adults actually learn and the fact that formal instruction is not the adult class's greatest strength.

I have changed my understanding of the relationship between *teaching* and *learning* for adults, and have come to believe that many, if not most, adult educators tend to confuse the two and do not see that they ought to stand quite apart. In this regard I have come to appreciate the great values of the so-called "lecture" and the severe limitation of group discussion as teaching methods for adults.

Four years of teaching adults and training workers with adults at First United Methodist Church, Houston, allowed me to try out many forms of adult education in that very large congregation. The insights of the pastor, Charles L. Allen, often caused me to think more clearly. Fifteen years of teaching courses on adults to young adults in a theological seminary, plus innumerable workshops and seminars throughout the country, have broadened my understanding a great deal. My children, Ruth and Martin, have taught me to understand the transition of youth to young adults and have helped me reflect on how that is done today. My colleagues in Christian education at Perkins School of Theology, Howard Grimes and Wayne Banks, as co-teachers and frequent challengers, have forced me to think more clearly and speak more moderately. Howard Grimes has patiently read and made suggestions on the manuscript.

Fleta Williams, administrative assistant in Continuing Education at Perkins, kept things organized while I studied and wrote. She also did research on the project and typed the manuscript. Her work has been invaluable.

Lyle E. Schaller urged me to do the writing and kept me at the job. Many of the statements made in this book have appeared in one or more of his books and in his regularly published *Parish Paper*. While in some cases he has suggested them to me, and occasionally vice versa, usually we have arrived at the same basic conclusions individually and have been pleased to find confirmation in the other's observations.

These persons are due great thanks, but are not responsible for anything that is said.

Introduction

The Protestant adult Sunday school class in the United States is a unique creature. It usually meets for an hour before the worship service on Sunday morning—occasionally after worship—and in some communities on Sunday afternoon. In some instances the classes have up to two hours for a session.

The class is primarily a lay movement, like the entire Sunday school, and the teachers have little, if any, formal training. Usually, the classes use curriculum resources provided by their own denominations, but the majority of them, in all denominations, still use the basic outlines of the International (Uniform) Lesson Series, first developed in 1872. In many instances these classes "use only the Bible" for their materials, ignoring the urging of their denomination.

Although they are called either "Adult Sunday School Classes" or "Adult Bible Classes," the first term will be used here to refer to both. In most churches only one-half to one-fourth of the adult members are enrolled in adult classes;

however, despite a drastic decline in enrollment and attendance in the last twenty years, several million adults are in classes every Sunday morning. If accurate figures were available, perhaps they would still show that more adults study in Sunday school than in any other facet of adult education in the country.

A large number of adult classes are found in the South and Southwest; fewer, but still strong, ones are in the Midwest; they are quite scarce in the Far West and Northeast. In some denominations this regional pattern does not prevail.

The classes are a blend of warm personal relationships, and an opportunity for members to grow spiritually through study and worship and to make a commitment to acts of service. Some critics feel that such classes concentrate on nothing, and thus do all things rather poorly. Many clergy are lukewarm about such classes and have always considered them a mixed blessing. Those who attend and lead them believe they are one of the most important parts of their lives.

Most books that have been published in recent years on this subject examine the entire field of adult Christian education, but here I will concentrate on the adult Sunday school class, usually lay taught, usually meeting on Sunday morning. We will pay scant attention to the many other forms of adult church education, such as short-term week night classes, classes taught by ministers at times other than Sunday morning, the adult education aspects of preaching and worship, or study groups of either a women's or men's organization.

All of these latter groups are of considerable importance in adult church education, possibly more important in many churches than the adult Sunday school classes.

It is the assumption of this book that while adult Sunday school classes fulfill a certain form of adult education, they have several other purposes and strengths which are of equal, or even greater, value. This has been true from the very early years of the adult class, certainly since the late 1800s, with the advent of the Baraca and Philathea classes which were the direct forerunners of the present-day adult class.

17

Ten Ways
to Strengthen Adult Classes
in Your Church

1. Accept the reality of what an adult class really is and build upon it. Help each class affirm its own life cycle and the persons it is likely to attract and serve.

2. Affirm the interplay of fellowship and learning and enhance the opportunity for both in adult classes.

3. Continually look for the opportunity to start new classes, knowing that they will not weaken the present classes. Study the present church membership, the constituency roll, and adult prospects in deciding which classes to organize.

4. Use the adult classes to serve the needs of the church by asking them to adopt missional priorities or to take on special local church needs with which they can feel personally identified.

5. Look for persons who will agree to teach an adult class for short periods of time, or at irregular times, to relieve the present teachers and allow all teachers a vacation regularly. Also seek out persons who will teach a particular subject, or portion of the Bible, and who will become "experts" in that particular area. They may teach *that* subject to several different adult classes over the years.

6. Strongly encourage *every* new adult member of the church to join an adult class and develop a system of follow-up to insure the best possible results. Assign responsibility to a specific class and possibly assign a specific couple or person to sponsor the newcomers for three months. This includes adults of *all* ages, married, widowed, or single.

7. Develop a plan of basic lay education in cooperation with the pastor, so that present and future teachers of adults may take courses in Bible, basic beliefs, church history, and application of the faith. Such courses will usually be taught in the evening for short periods of time (six to ten weeks).

8. Periodically, conduct a class for new adult members, or persons considering membership, in which the basic doctrines

of the Christian faith are reviewed. Ask representatives of the adult classes to host this class and to invite and steer participants toward an appropriate adult class when the class is concluded.

9. Develop a plan of encouraging and enabling adult classes to reach out into the community to witness to their faith and to invite unchurched persons to visit their class and the church. Have occasional sessions for adult teachers and class officers to discuss ways to witness in our time and to offer opportunities for personal commitments.

10. Publicize the life of the adult classes from the pulpit, in the church newsletter, and by other means, holding up things that are done which are unusual or especially valuable. Do not assume, even in a small church, that persons in the membership at large are aware of the special course of study in one class, or of a special service project, or of a new plan to enlist new class members.

I
Myths and Realities

In this book, myth is used in the conventional "street" sense, which assumes that a myth is essentially not true. In theology, myth is often used to refer to a story that conveys a profound truth, which can *only* be put in story form.

The myths that form the structure of this book are statements which are assumed to be true by a certain group of people, sometimes by church professionals, sometimes by laypersons in general, sometimes by denominational educational leaders—at times by professors in seminaries or universities.

In each case, I have come to believe that while the myth points to some truth, it is *essentially* false and should not be depended upon to understand reality. The myths are, therefore, used as vehicles to point to what I consider to be the more important truths, an understanding of which is important in improving what we do in church education for adults.

Two Approaches to Adult Classes

Throughout this book I will refer to two basic approaches to adult Sunday school classes—ongoing and short-term.

The Ongoing Class

This is a class that is usually made up of people more or less the same age, and sometimes the same sex or marital status, who expect to remain in that class *indefinitely*. The focus of the class is the class itself, not the subject that is being studied at any particular time. Fellowship within such classes is very strong, class officers are usually important, and the class engages in acts of service, as well as study.

It would be rare for members of such classes to think of their membership as a lifelong commitment, but in actuality it is. Of course, over the years new persons join the class; so the composition changes, but the expectation is that members won't change classes, or just drop out. Many persons do drop out for a variety of reasons, and others change classes, but it takes a good deal of personal courage to do either.

The Short-Term Class

This is a class that is announced for a limited period of time—anything from a few weeks to three months, six months, or, at times, a year. The focus of the class is a subject to be studied which will be dealt with in a set period of time. Such classes usually are not grouped according to age, sex, or marital status, and, therefore, include a diverse group of persons who often hardly know one another. Short-term classes often have only a teacher, or leader, no class officers at all, and rarely any social events or service projects.

In either of these types the personality of the teacher may be a very important reason that persons join that class.

Knowing About and Knowing Of

It is the point of view of this book that the church has always struggled between the relative values of knowing *about* the

21

faith and knowing *of* the faith. The Sunday school is quite successful in helping persons know *of* the faith, but it does so in the guise and framework of knowing *about* the faith. This fact is often missed or ignored.

This author further believes that the framework of knowing *about* is one of the good ways to increase knowing *of,* and that it is, in fact, often more successful than a frontal attack to simply know *of.* This is true because a direct, "Do you love Jesus?" approach easily becomes shallow and sentimental, while seeking a response to the same question in the context of a portion of the tradition (biblical narrative, for instance) can give some substance to the response.

On the other hand, a preoccupation with knowing about a certain body of material often diverts one from expressing one's emotions or commitments, and the question, "Do you love Jesus?" becomes a total embarrassment.

The educational and evangelistic emphasis of the church, and its respective enthusiasts, have pushed and pulled on this issue, often unknowingly, and the Sunday school has been caught in the middle.

Thus, shall we *instruct* or shall we *nurture* continues to be a major issue. *My response is, we should instruct in a manner which is open and conducive to nurture, knowing that nurture, or enculturation, is, in fact, our major goal and product.*

As to how we do this, the answer is sometimes in context, other times in point of view, and sometimes in method. In this section we will try to reflect on all of these and show how they interact.

Christian leaders want the persons with whom they work to have an *educated faith.* They believe that such a faith will, in the long run, stand up better to the strains and stresses of life than "only an emotional faith."

What is an educated faith? Basically, education is a process by which a phenomenon is seen in perspective. Thus, an educated Christian would be exposed in some detail to the basic documents and narratives of the faith. This is, in fact, true of many Christians. But, an educated person is also aware of the fundamental questions the faith tries to answer: What kinds of answers have various groups offered in the past? Why have they given *those* answers? How do these relate to the answers others have made to the same questions? Few Christians have much exposure to this latter process.

Would the church be able to fulfill its calling decisively if it could educate its masses in this fashion?

We have very little hard evidence to support a yes answer. Throughout the centuries, the more educated a particular branch of the church becomes, the less drive it has to either *win* or *serve* humankind.

But, it is also essential to remember that certain persons who become immersed in the faith *have to* educate themselves to satisfy the calling of the faith within. In a real sense, education is *for* the individual who desires it and satisfies his/her own demands "to know."

The question before the educated then becomes, As I learn more and more *about* God, how can I grow in my knowledge *of* God?

The answer of the Sunday school to that question is: through the depth of personal relationships, in experiencing the vicissitudes of life in the presence of the witness of the Christian faith. This is where the Sunday school's strength lies.

What It Really Is

"I belong to this class because I believe that every week I grow spiritually."

"Both the inspiring lessons and the wonderful spirit of the class make me feel it is one of the most worthwhile things I do."

Above all else, this is what I hear from class members who belong to ongoing classes. Spiritual growth, strengthened faith, a deepened and enriched life, coupled with a feeling of being a part of a caring, vital group—that is why they come. Fellowship and group warmth are not enough—nor is an "interesting and informative lesson." It is the combination that makes the experience so important.

23

1.
Myth
The Sunday school is a real school.

Reality
The Sunday school is a school of faith in which persons share with one another the stories of the faith and interact with one another in concern and love. This is done in the name of Jesus Christ as a response to the love of God.

This is what the Sunday school *is* and *has been* in the past, but it is sometimes hard to remember.

The Sunday school started in England in the mid-to-late eighteenth century and soon spread to the United States. Started by laypersons outside the structure of the church for children from poor families, the earliest Sunday schools stressed reading and writing as well as religion.

But the Sunday school soon became allied with the organized church and shifted its emphasis to teaching the Bible and the catechism, and the children of church families became participants. Emphasis has *always* been on the witness of the faithful to secure commitments to the Christian life. Thus, evangelism—witnessing to the good news—has been important in the Sunday school, although that emphasis has faded today in several mainline churches.

I do not know when adult classes first became a part of the Sunday school, but I believe it was much earlier than is commonly thought. Certainly there were adult Bible classes led by clergy and laypersons in the eighteenth century, and before 1815 adult classes were organized in several Sunday schools in New England.

I believe these first adult classes became Sunday school classes when a brave and trusting preacher said to an uncertain layperson, "You teach the class and I'll do something else." Such groups met at various times, and then moved to Sunday and met at the same time as the classes for children.

When you think of an adult Sunday school class you need to redefine both the word *school* and the word *class*. They do not fit the images of the public school or other educational institutions. In the Sunday school there are no standards for admission, no professional teachers, no assignments or tests to be graded, and none of the other accepted procedures for a public school or class.

But this does not mean that *learning*—learning the Christian faith, and commitment—commitment to the Christian faith— do not take place! It is not instruction but *nurture* which the Sunday school does best. Instruction does take place, but it is in a context of sharing and witnessing which overshadows the data.

Mrs. Pickford was my primary Sunday school teacher. I do not remember the lessons she taught. Mrs. Pickford I remember *very* well. She was gracious, understanding, and warm. She made all of us feel valuable and able. Her only problem, as I remember it, was being naïve. She kept saying she was sure I wouldn't do anything wrong, when I knew all along I was fully planning to do so. The strange thing is, I often proved her right because I couldn't "let her down"!

We developed this relationship during the weekly lesson—a lesson I do not remember but a lesson about some story of the faith that strengthened our relationship. This is Christian nurture.

I have never met anyone who has been willing to say, "When you have learned these things, you will be a Christian," or, "If you don't know this thing, you are not a Christian."

Rather, Christians talk of "knowing Jesus" or "knowing God," but no specific body of information is tied to either phrase. Instead, the process of coming to know God is tied to the interaction we have with those who believe they have come to know him, as we listen together to the stories of the faithful from scripture and history.

25

The Sunday school is a unique school—a school in which we tell stories, share life, seek answers to the deepest questions, and laugh at one another's joy and cry at one another's pain—not a "real" school—but possibly the most *real-real* school there can be.

2.
Myth
Adults attend Sunday school classes primarily to learn.

Reality
When questioned adults say they attend adult classes: "Because of the fellowship in the group." "To strengthen my faith." "To grow spiritually." "To hear a fine teacher." "To go somewhere while the children are in Sunday school."

What It Is

The ongoing adult Sunday school class must realistically be thought of as a church-organized social group, which incorporates to some extent all the ministries of the church: worship, study, fellowship, witness, outreach, and service. In truth, such classes have acted like "little churches," and for some persons have actually become the church. In the adult class, the leadership is entirely in lay hands, and usually no one present has any theological education. This has been, and continues to be, both its strength and its weakness.

Most adult classes meet formally for an hour. At least half, and sometimes two-thirds, of the hour is devoted to the lesson. It would appear to someone making a casual observation that the lesson was the reason the people were there. It is true, I believe, that without the lesson, the group would not exist, but its reasons for being are far greater than study and learning.

The one hour for class is actually deceptive, because often a half hour before and fifteen to twenty minutes afterward are used by class members for casual talking. (See myth number ten.) Thus, many adult classes use about *two hours* each Sunday morning, of which the lesson takes less than half of the time. In some churches, a half-hour department period of fellowship and worship is prior to the class meetings.

Adults come for a multitude of reasons, which may be quite different from what they will receive. Many men go to please their wives, or to placate them. This does not mean that once there they will not enjoy the fellowship, be stimulated by the lesson, and be challenged to serve. It simply means that if their wives didn't push, the husbands wouldn't go! The same may be said of many other honest reasons for going which don't seem to be very worthy on their own, but may result in a very positive experience.

The kind of ministry and the amount of time spent on it varies with each class but real care shown to individual members is found to some extent in all of them.

Discipleship: Caring/Sharing

One of the major ways to serve God is to love and care for one's neighbor. This is one thing the ongoing adult Sunday school class does best.

To the question, "How is Sally this week?" one member reports, "Well, I talked to her on Tuesday." "I went by on Thursday—took her a warm dish," says another. "She seems to be holding her own, but does not have the motivation to cook anything." Another says, "I believe we ought to work out

27

a plan to take her something at least twice a week." So it goes, as a typical adult class cares—not casually, but with thought, planning, and sustained concern—which makes a significant impact on the life of this person.

Sally recovers and returns to the class. As she takes part in the lessons, either listening to a lecture or participating in a discussion, she does so in the context of the caring and sharing which the class takes for granted. Her learning is different because of the loving community of which she is a part. *This is a context for learning which is quite unique in the American scene.*

The Baraca Bible Class for young men was started at the First Baptist Church of Syracuse, New York, in 1890. Baraca means "blessed" or "happy," and the stated aim of the class was "to make happy every young man who comes within our circle" ○. While such a goal *can* result in very superficial handshaking and pretense at good cheer, it can also end in the kind of care Sally, and millions of others, receive.

A pastor in a small town describes the fellowship found in the classes of her church:

> There's an incredible sense of "belonging" within the older classes, especially. For example, persons may not attend class for months, maybe years, but they are still called "active" members. Or, they attend the monthly socials, which the Friendship and Dorcas classes do regularly. Fellowship Class gathers quarterly. The Men's Bible Class goes to ball games together.

Major criticism of ongoing adult classes are: they can become self-centered, are only interested in their own, and make it almost impossible for a newcomer to "break into the group." It is true that this happens, and every class needs challenges to draw it out and help its members become aware of more distant needs and ways they can be met.

It *is* quite easy for any social group, such as an adult Sunday school class, to become preoccupied with itself. This usually happens, interestingly enough, without the class members being aware of it, and most of them would strongly deny it. This happens because the class members *feel* a strong desire to take in new people and to care for and serve persons at a distance, but the pleasures of being a part of an intimate group simply blind them to the realities of their behavior. Mary enters the room and immediately sees familiar persons with whom she wants to talk. When someone says, "Mary, meet our visitors, Walter and Betty," she will greet them, chat a minute, and then turn back to the familiar group. It is not indifference—it is simply the powerful attraction of friends well known.

Thus, it takes conscious effort to "keep the door really open" so that the *outsider* can have a real chance of becoming an *insider*. Many class members will extend the "caring circle" personally and automatically, but a system is also required. One common and important practice is to have name tags for everyone. In a class where "everybody knows everybody," this may seem a waste of time, but it can be *very* important for the visitors, or newcomers, to help them get acquainted.

Systemic Caring

Many people come to adult classes because of the caring relationships. For this reason, most classes need organization and someone to coordinate the attention paid to persons. If hot dishes are to be taken to a shut-in, there is no point in everyone taking them on the same day! It is important that such activities not become mechanical, but it is also important that they are done. Southern Baptists suggest a group leader for every three to four persons in a class, and other churches call this responsibility by a variety of names.

The Whole Person's Whole Life

One of the major values of the Sunday school and of the adult Sunday school class is its interest in the *whole person for his/her whole life.* This is a place where you can come and stay until you die with people who care. As you come, you will be surrounded by persons like yourself for whom *you* can care. Together weekly you will look into the scriptures and to God for the challenge of the needy neighbor and the strength to be of help.

II
Myths and Realities of Organization

3.
Myth
Adult classes can stay young
(while their members grow older).

Reality
By and large, adult classes attract persons only
a few years younger than the youngest charter
members, and nearly all ongoing adult classes
die within a few years following the death of the
last charter member. This is emphatically true of
couples' classes and is somewhat less true of
singles' classes and men's Bible classes, al-
though they die, too.

The significance of this is: the efforts made by existing classes to block the starting of new classes of younger persons, because "they will take our prospects," are a waste of time. These younger persons are, in fact, not real *prospects for the present class.*

Ongoing Classes Have Life Cycles

One of the difficult things for many persons active in ongoing adult classes is to realize that their class will die. Unlike churches, adult classes, by and large, do not go on generation after generation, but instead have a life cycle of usefulness. This life cycle varies with different kinds of adult classes.

The men's Bible class movement was at its peak during the late 1800s and early 1900s, but now most men's Bible classes are made up of men in their seventies and eighties and are declining in size. Why? There are many reasons. Mixed classes of men and women—both married couples and mixed singles—have become far more popular than a few years ago. Dividing by age is now much more widespread than dividing by sex, and this is even moving into Southern Baptist Sunday schools where mixed classes are now quite common.

But the other and major factor is the fact that few classes attract persons who are more than ten years younger than their average age.

Couples' classes became popular right after World War I, and in the early 1920s many classes of young couples were started for the first time in our churches. Typically, such groups consisted of a few couples in their early twenties, most without children. Couples who joined such classes stayed in them all their lives and now, in 1980, they are an average of eighty years old. As might be expected, many of those classes are deciding now either to merge with other classes, stop meeting entirely, or have monthly or quarterly social gatherings.

Can anyone consider this to be bad? The persons who remain, of course, regret that their class does not have the vigor of the past, but they can be proud that it and other classes like it have had a *very fruitful history*.

A Typical Class Life Cycle

In their *childhood* these classes provided a spiritual base for the members as they started their marriages, had their first children, developed confidence in their jobs, and began to assume positions of responsibility in the community. The first teachers were more mature men and women whom they admired, and often, unconsciously, used as role models.

As the members grew into their thirties and left their young adult years, many of these classes had an exuberant *adolescence*. The members now knew one another well, most had two to four children in elementary school, and were well settled in their marriages and jobs. Some couples got divorces, and often one of the former partners remained active in the class where he or she received a lot of personal support.

Baseball games, picnics, and other family events in which the children could be included were popular, and endless hours were spent on significant projects for worthy causes. Many of the members took turns as teachers in the children's classes.

Sometimes the women in the classes formed a women's auxiliary or subgroups for Bible study, "42," or bridge, when such classes became larger than fifty.

The children of the class members became a real community of their own, and friendships were formed which led to much dating in later years, and even to a few marriages.

In the forties and fifties the couples' classes entered into their *maturity*. Now the members had taken over many of the key jobs in the organizational life of the church. They also were major contributors to the budget and leaders in the wider community. Their children moved through rather painful teen-age years. During this time many members of the class felt that they would never have made it without the insights, friendly tears, and encouragement of the other class members. Every marriage in the class suffered certain strains, more divorces occurred, and on occasion, a divorce and marriage would result which would cause a mild scandal. Several class members died, especially the men, and on Sunday mornings there might be 20 percent more women than men in the class.

As most of the class members move into their sixties to seventies, attendance usually drops as more members die, or become unable to attend. Nevertheless, this class serves newcomers of the same age span who feel at home with grandparents like themselves. Most of the employed persons in the class retire in these years, many quite reluctantly, while others look forward to travel and the enjoyment of several hobbies.

For many persons, the class becomes even more important to them than in their earlier years, for some are left alone when a husband or wife dies, and others have less to do because of retirement. Social activities change, but at times increase, as do projects in which the members really get involved. Usually, the members now have more time than money to contribute. Younger persons, usually the children of class members, take over most of the official positions in the church, and the class feels both relief and a little left out.

The final stage in the life cycle of such a class occurs as most members celebrate birthdays in their eighties and a few in their nineties. In these years, class attendance drops sharply, and the morale of the class is not good. It is now in a room far larger than is needed, and the church is quietly urging it to move to a smaller space. Many members can come only if they are brought, and that becomes increasingly difficult.

Often the class merges with another class during this period, but the new group rarely "feels right" for many in the former groups, and attendance is less than before. Other classes vote to stop meeting on Sunday morning but to continue to meet monthly, or less often, for dinner and a get-together. Actually,

33

more persons come to these meetings than had come to Sunday school for several years! A few classes continue to meet on Sundays with only two or three in attendance, especially if the "old teacher" is still there.

Several things must be said about the fifty to seventy years of such a class:

First, *thank God!* A good life—well done, over a long pull.

Second, it is essential that several new classes for younger persons have been started over the years as this class has gone through its life.

Third, prospects for *this* class have probably moved into the community every year. They are the persons who were of the same general age of this class at this time—not much younger and not much older. Also, this class continues to be attractive and valuable to their neighbors and fellow workers.

Fourth, the realities of such a life span need to be interpreted to this class periodically, so it will not fight desperately "to stay young" and will not become discouraged with its changing situation.

4.
Myth

There are lots of prospects for our classes in the church membership. Only one-fourth of the adults in our church belong to one of our classes.

Reality

*There are virtually **no** prospects for any of the existing adult classes in the present membership of the church. Efforts to recruit them are a great waste of time.*

Prospects for the existing classes are all outside the present membership of the church. Organizing new classes is the only real way to get present church members into a class.

Church Members in No Adult Class

At the peak period of Sunday school enrollment in the late 1950s, fewer than one-fourth of the adult church members in most mainline Protestant churches belonged to an adult class. Of course, in most cases, the larger the church, the smaller the percentage. Many of those who are not members are former members of one of the present classes, or former members of a class in another church. Why do they not come anymore? Although it is often difficult to dig out the truth, one of the primary reasons is personal dissatisfaction with the leaders in their former group. It has been said very truthfully, *"One of the major reasons people don't go to Sunday school is because of the people who do."*

The natural Christian response is that it should not be that way! But, it is, largely because of the very strength of the Sunday school class—its closeness and personal intimacy.

Other adults in the church tried out several classes soon after joining the church but did not feel that they "fit" in any of them, and said, "They simply were not our kind of folk," or, "They were so interested in themselves they hardly knew we were there."

It is a well-established fact that adults who do not join an adult class in the first six months after joining the church are likely not to do so. This is certainly true after the first year of membership, unless there is some major change in their lives, such as the death of a husband or wife, or the development of strong personal friendships with persons who are very active in a class.

A third group are those adults whose intellectual or spiritual needs do not seem to be met by any class in the church. This

35

may be based on difference in theological understanding or in a special quest for depth in prayer or critical Bible study.

Recently, I was visiting with a couple who have gone to Sunday school all their lives, but until recently, had never felt "at home" in an adult class. They enthusiastically talked of their unique class of about twelve persons, ranging in age from late twenties to early seventies. They have no regular teacher—rotating the leadership. Virtually everyone reads the lesson material every week, plus a commentary or two. The discussions are informative and spirited. They said they "often get in pretty deep"—which they all love to do.

None of these persons would ever go back to their former classes. They were waiting for this *new* class that "fit them" to start.

A fourth group of adult church members "wouldn't be caught dead in a Sunday school class. I had enough of that as a child!" They will never join a class even though they may engage in serious study in other ways.

Starting New Classes

In our survey of four hundred churches throughout the country we asked how new classes were started. Here are a few of the responses:

"The Open Door Class was started because our adult classes (three) had become large and people did not feel they had the opportunity to really know one another. Several couples in already established classes asked to start a new class. A teacher was secured, and the class began to meet with six couples. It has grown to forty members."

"Our younger couples' class grew out of a study of our church membership and our total adult ministry by our adult coordinator."

"The Crusaders' Class was organized to fill the need of women who were widows, or whose husbands were enrolled in the men's Bible class, or who had no specific class to attend. At first the class met in the last two or three pews in the back of the church and later moved to the chapel, where it is now meeting."

One of the most important principles in starting new classes is to be sure that a class of that type is needed.

In many instances, a church needs one or more new classes of the same type or age it already has, rather than needing a class for a group who do not attend your church. (See myth number nine.)

A Good, Solid Way to Start a New Class

1. Carefully go over the records of the church membership, comparing it to adult class membership, and see in which age groups there are several prospects. Also go over the constituency roll (those who are prospects, or who look to your church as their church). Decide on a group to invite to a new class.
2. Personally contact or telephone several of the persons on your list, tell them about the plans for the new class, and ask for their commitment to be charter members. *Do not proceed further unless you get several commitments*—switch to another group.
3. Secure a teacher for the first three months, with a clear agreement that either the class or the teacher may change at that time.
4. Choose study materials for the first three months.
5. Ask the minister (senior minister) to write a letter to all the persons on the prospect list inviting them to a dessert meeting, preferably at the parsonage. It must be remembered that some of these persons who attend only the worship service, know only the preacher very well.

   Ask the persons who have already agreed to join the class to divide up the list and telephone every person so they will receive both a letter and a call.
6. At the meeting, announce that the class will meet next Sunday in such and such a room. Introduce the temporary teacher and the first curriculum. Also introduce the persons already committed to join. Invite everyone to come on Sunday.

   (Do not, at any time, ask the persons if they *want* such a class. Assume that they do.)

7. Expect one-half to one-third of the group the first Sunday. Call, or visit, those who do not come at least twice.

When class members ask, "Where are the prospects for our class?" the answer is always basically the same. The persons who are likely to become active in your class are the persons with whom your present members are in contact, who are not members of any local church, and who feel that they are like most of your members. Other prospects for your class are newcomers to your community who, also, can come to believe that your class is made up of persons with whom they can share many interests.

Whether your class is made up primarily of couples in their twenties or women in their eighties, the answer is the same. The persons who are likely to join your class are those persons with whom your class members work, with whom they bowl or play tennis, who belong to their clubs, who are related to them, or who move into their neighborhoods. Those of this number who say to themselves after visiting the class, "Those are my kind of folk," are the ones who are likely to join. Interestingly enough, many adults are ready to cross denominational lines to find such a group.

Some Christians who are repelled by this homogeneous approach to adult class participation, look for groups of varied age, race, social class, and theological perspective. Such varied classes do exist and are very helpful to their members, but they are relatively rare across the country.

Age has proved, over the long run, to be the most consistently useful way to divide adults. Whether requiring movement to a new class every five years (as in many Southern Baptist Sunday Schools), or simply having an informal clustering of persons over a twenty-year age span, age grouping is very attractive to most adults.

Thus, persons of the same general age are the best prospects for an ongoing class. The class of women in their eighties will often do more to minister to an eighty-year-old newcomer to the community than any other group. Of course, each of those persons want, and need, other relationships with much younger persons in a variety of circumstances, such as they had known in their families. Perhaps the church can do some things, other than worship, across generational lines, but the Sunday school class is rarely one of them.

5.
Myth
Small churches need only one adult class.

Reality
Even in a very small congregation it is difficult to get three generations to attend the same class. Usually, part of the second generation, and most of the third generation, stay away.

A second class for younger adults is very desirable in the small church. The primary problems are: the resistance of the older class and the need for teachers of the children and youth.

There are many kinds of small churches, each of which has its own problems and opportunities.

Here we will look at adult classes in two types of small churches which share some characteristics, but are quite different in other ways:

The small rural or urban church, which often is static, or declining in membership.

The brand new, small suburban church, which is just starting, possibly meeting in a school.

Small Rural or Urban Church

The key issue in the small church is *the maximum use of its available resources.* This is especially true of its members, as the church seeks to live and move into the future with hope. It is not likely that there will be a large influx of newcomers (although this is happening in a number of places), so the persons who are there, in the community, are the ones who are going to be the church.

In many instances we are talking about some six to ten families, who have lived in the community a long time, have intermarried, and represent at least three generations, possibly four. There is a general pattern of the young people leaving the community after finishing high school and bringing their families back to visit.

In many of these churches there is *one* adult class for all who come, primarily persons over fifty. It meets in one corner of the sanctuary and is taught by the same person who has done it for many years. In a few instances, there is a women's class and a men's class, but in the last several years these have usually merged. In the most vigorous of such churches there is a younger class for adults, generally under thirty-five, which allows daughters to be in a different class from their mothers and grandmothers. *Having such a class for younger adults seems to be a key to continuing strength of leadership in the church and is highly desirable.*

There are usually only three or four couples in the community who are prospects for such a class, and possibly a single person, or two. This means that several of these persons are regularly called upon to teach the classes of children, or youth, and it is quite possible that attendance in this class can easily average fewer than four or five. This is hard on morale, and such classes often come and go, and do not develop real strength.

Several solutions to this problem have been developed, three of which are listed here:

1. A regular rotation system is developed so that no person is asked to teach a children's class over three months at a time, allowing the short-term teacher to return to the adult class. Since the children know *all* the adults quite well, the problem of personal identification is not great. In this pattern it is very helpful if men are included in the

regular rotation. Other patterns of rotation are also used successfully.

2. Since there are often only two or three youth (twelve to seventeen) in the community, it is a great struggle to have a youth class. At times, these youth prefer to teach or help with the children's classes than to struggle with a class of their own. Often such a group can travel to other churches on Sunday evening and during the week for their own youth fellowship. *We have greatly underestimated the need and opportunity to use youth in significant service.* Of course, this plan can be combined with the first.

3. In some small churches, it seems impossible to have the younger adult class on Sunday morning—so it meets on Sunday evening, or some other night of the week. It is still called a Sunday school class and does the same things, but meets at a time other than Sunday morning when its members are often committed to teach.

While none of these solutions is perfect, they do work, and having a younger adult class is usually very valuable. While the generations get along fairly well, they have radically different problems and life-styles, and they need a chance to face life with their age peers as they attempt to interpret the Christian faith for themselves.

Newly Organized Small Urban Churches

When a new congregation starts in a suburb of a city, or some other area where a denomination thinks there ought to be a new church, there is a strong tendency to ignore adult Sunday school classes. Emphasis is almost entirely on the worship service (as it should be) and on starting Sunday school classes for children and youth. Nevertheless, there is considerable evidence that when provision is made for adult Sunday school at the very beginning, the resulting church is strengthened.

One method that has been very successful is to have the worship service first, followed by Sunday school. After a coffee break between, the adults assemble in the place they have just worshiped (school gym, or other place), sit in groups of six to ten to be led by a prepared leader in a discussion of the key ideas of the sermon just heard. Often the minister will meet with the leaders during the week to help them prepare for the discussion.

After a twenty- to thirty-minute period of discussion, the minister often comes in and questions from one or more of the groups are asked, or comments are made to him. Sometimes a very spirited, general discussion will follow.

Some churches keep this type of adult class for the first year, or more, and then form several permanent ongoing classes from this class, utilizing some of the leaders who developed during the initial period. This requires that the new church is continuing to grow and the number of adults are continuing to increase.

Another successful way to begin an adult class in a newly formed church is for the minister to teach the class, and use it as a leadership development group for the emerging church. In such a situation, many adults are often young and inexperienced in the church, and some are from different denominational backgrounds.

They *need* and *want* information on the basics of the Christian faith, the key beliefs and practices of that denomination, as well as the chance to get to know one another as persons. They also need to know the minister and he/she needs to know them better. Eventually, this class may form one or two new groups by age, or interest, that can move out on their own.

A third pattern in a new congregation is to form adult classes as soon as possible on the basis of interest or subject matter. One new church reached one hundred members in a little over a month and organized two adult classes, which met in the corners of the school auditorium where worship services were held. One class studied the Bible, while the other worked on basic beliefs and theology. Both of these classes had regular teachers who had had experience teaching adults in other churches. A third class was formed in another two months. Its members discussed a wide variety of subjects and rotated the leadership around the class.

In all these cases, the new congregation made adult classes a part of its life very early, and thus had a Sunday school for the entire family from the beginning.

6.
Myth
Ongoing adult classes are best.

Reality
Each type of class has its own benefits and liabilities and needs to be affirmed for what it does best.

The ongoing adult class provides a depth of community and possibility for informal— "survival"—education far better than the short-term class.

The short-term adult class provides strong subject-focused adult learning which often speaks directly, instructively, and powerfully to an immediate felt-need or crisis. There are some real values in not knowing the members of the class too well—providing an avenue for free exchange of ideas and feelings without too much fear of damaging relationships.

Ideally, most adults will participate in both types of groups regularly.

The Regionalism of Adult Classes

For reasons that I cannot fully fathom, *ongoing* adult Sunday school classes are largely a regional phenomenon in the United States today. Throughout the Southeast and Southwest, and to a large extent in the north central states, you will find many of these classes for adults. In the Northeast, Northwest, and Far West, in general, there are few adult classes which persons join and stay in all their lives. At least this is true in the so-called mainline denominations.

Part of the explanation for this reality is that Sunday schools, and churches in general, are stronger in the same regions of the country which also have a high proportion of WASPS (White, Anglo-Saxon Protestants) in the population. Southern Baptist and Pentecostal churches seem to transcend this regionalism to a large extent.

In the mid 1800s, the first and largest Sunday schools and adult classes were in such cities as Philadelphia, Pennsylvania, and Brooklyn, New York. There has been a very large shift in the last one hundred years, or so. In 1949 I was appointed to two small churches in New York state, on the Hudson River, and discovered that neither had had any adult classes for at least thirty years. Over a four-year pastorate we did a wide variety of things in adult education in both churches, but we were never able to start an adult Sunday morning class.

In response to my recent survey of adult classes, I received this reply from Massachusetts: "In New England adult ongoing Sunday school classes have generally disappeared (about eighty years ago, I guess). The best I've been able to do is a year's program of short-term courses on week days, or afternoons, and occasional forums on Sunday mornings."

From what I can learn, the best way to involve adults in church education in areas where there are few ongoing classes is to have short-term classes by subject on Sunday morning, or during the week.

Values of Short-Term Classes

The limitations of ongoing adult classes became very evident in the 1940s and 1950s, and several denominations tried to close down such classes and replace them with short-term, subject-based classes. The ongoing classes were charged with being ingrown, interested only in themselves and cool to newcomers, hero worshipers of the teacher, and a "church" within the church, as well as not seriously studying the lesson. In many instances, such accusations were true, but the virtues and values of the classes were often ignored. Unfortunately, the emphasis on short-term classes often discouraged attendance, and overall adult enrollment dropped drastically where short-term classes were most successful.

Nevertheless, there are major advantages in the short-term course concept.

For one thing, many adults prefer not being committed to an ongoing class, especially in this time of great mobility. Further, a variety of curriculum resources can be used and completed in a period of weeks, with a sense of accomplishment, which is often missing in an ongoing class. If a person signs up for a new subject every few weeks, in a new class, he/she has the opportunity to get acquainted with a different group of people, as well as to be under the leadership of a different teacher. Most importantly, he/she can choose the subjects he/she is interested in studying. This allows the adult to be in charge of another factor in his/her own learning.

Many churches have gone to this approach because of a real slump in their old classes. A pastor at a five-hundred membership church in south Texas says, "In the spring of 1978, our three adult classes had dwindled in attendance until we had only a few people who were interested in attending, and we could not recruit a teacher for any of them. Two were couples' classes, and one was a recently formed class for senior adults." After forming a representative study group to reconsider the entire adult education program, the pastor continues, "What emerged was an enthusiastic group that decided to disband all of the previous classes and to establish our adult education program on a quarterly basis, in which all adults would be able to choose 'university' style, what course they would like to enroll in for the upcoming quarter."

This church tried four courses a quarter, at first, then dropped to three, and finally to two, because that was all that could be supported by adequate attendance. During the summer they change format, one class with a different teacher each Sunday. They also found that recruiting a full year of teachers can be done best during the summer and that several persons *were* willing to teach for a limited time on a given subject.

Most denominations provide a variety of such short-term courses (up to a quarter—thirteen weeks) in length. Write to your denominational Board of Education for full information.

Both Ongoing and Short-Term

A few churches have several ongoing classes, and, on occasion, offer short-term classes as well on Sunday morning. In a number of cases, pastors report that the ongoing classes felt this procedure was too *competitive,* so the short-term courses were dropped on Sunday morning and offered at other times during the week.

The most commonly reported Sunday morning short-term classes were courses conducted by the pastor for new, or prospective, members, usually running four to six weeks in length, and often held two or three times a year. These are very successful and serve to introduce newcomers to the various adult classes, which many of them join after the new members' class is concluded.

When I was on the staff of First United Methodist Church, Houston, Texas, we ran such a class for a four-week sequence, but had enough newcomers to conduct it over and over again, without a break, except in the summer.

In other churches, the education committee plans at least one Sunday morning short-term course each fall and spring. One church I know had a six-week class on "Religion and

Mental Health," two sessions each, taught by three local doctors. There were no available classrooms, so the class met in the small balcony of the sanctuary. About half of the forty who attended came from one of the existing seven ongoing classes, while the rest were persons who attended no adult class at all. The church considered this very worthwhile and offered such courses regularly for several years.

Both ongoing and short-term adult classes have real, but often different, values.

7.
Myth
*Classes should not get too large.
Small classes are far more intimate
and personal.*

Reality
*Many adult classes with over one hundred
members—even two hundred to three hundred—
have a great sense of concern for each person and
have enthusiastic subgroups in which persons
find identity.*

*Subdividing a strong class often means that
one-half will remain vital but the other group
will have a very hard time. Certainly there must
be great interest in and commitment to the
division within the class for it to succeed.*

How Close Is Too Close?

When I go to the post office window in the small town where I am writing, and the clerk says, "Good morning, Mr. Murray," I feel known and warm inside. This is an important feeling for everyone, and we all need some place to go where that will happen. For a great many that happens in an adult Sunday school class.

On the other hand, it is possible to be in a group (often a class) where everyone knows everyone else *so well* that little, if anything, is ever private. If the granddaughter of a class member has a spat with her husband, it is known by every member of the class in a few days, even though the couple live several hundred miles away!

Two things must always be kept in mind. First, everyone needs both intimacy *and* distance. Second, individuals differ in the proportions of intimacy and distance which they desire. Therefore, there is always an important place for both large and small churches, and large and small adult classes. Wherever possible, every church should provide an opportunity for both.

"Small" Does Not Equal Concern

Many people believe that a teacher who can call every class member by name will automatically be more concerned about each person and will, therefore, be a better teacher than one who is not that close to each individual. This is hardly true. Some people are far more adept than others at remembering names, but personal concern runs far deeper than that.

A few years ago I was a member of a large class with an attendance of ninety. The teacher was a person who knew his subject very well and was extremely excited about its implications for life and the Christian faith. There was no chance for this teacher to get to know each of us personally, nor for all of us to get to know one another.

Nevertheless, the spirit of the teacher was that of ultimate concern and interest in every person. Whenever a question was raised, or a comment was made, the teacher indicated to all of us that he was truly listening and that no one was being ignored, or neglected.

The spirit and attitude of the class and the teacher are more important in developing concern than the size of the class.

When Is a Class Too Large?

I recently surveyed about twenty adult classes of various sizes (1980), and asked the question, "When is an adult class too large?" Here are a number of typical responses:

"When it is too large to relate to a majority of its members."
"When someone comes and doesn't get recognized or spoken to."
"When the class doesn't need my volunteer service."
"When there are more people that I don't know than I do know."
"When the class can't fit into one home for socials."
"When it is hard to hear the speaker."
"When all cannot participate in lesson discussion."

In terms of actual numbers, the responses varied from "never too large," to as low as fifteen.

In my survey, it was always true that the smaller the class—the smaller the members thought a class should be, and conversely, the larger the class, the larger the members thought the class should be. This shows, of course, that persons liked either a small or large class, depending on the kind in which they were enrolled.

Some denominations have a firm policy of trying to restrict the size of adult classes to a group that can fully engage in discussion (fifteen to twenty). This is true of the Southern Baptist Church, but my observation is that the benefits of a large class are obtained by their very active adult departments, which have from a few (two or three) classes to as many as twenty.

There is no doubt that many adults prefer a very large class. There are several reasons. They want to be known, but not too well. They do not want to be asked to respond to questions, or take part in a class discussion. They want to "hear a really good

49

teacher who knows more than I do." They want to feel a part of a large, successful, enthusiastic organization. They like the variety of persons they find in a large group.

I believe that most churches should have *at least one class* that grows as large as it can, with several small discussion classes for those who prefer them.

Dividing a Large Class

Dividing a class is initiated either from the inside (by class members, or officers) or from the outside by the pastor or committee on education. Such division is desired for a variety of reasons. Possibly attendance is *very poor* in relation to membership. Or, the age spread has become very broad, possibly thirty to forty years. At times, persons in charge simply believe that classes "should not be that large." Sometimes the class has gained so much power in the congregation that the "tail is wagging the dog." Often newcomers visit the class but do not join, because they say "it is too large and impersonal."

What should be done?

As a general rule it is always better to start new classes around the large one (attracting some persons out of it), than dividing the present class by a rather bloody process of surgery.

Nevertheless, large classes *can* be divided successfully, especially if carried out from the inside, rather than exclusively from the outside. The division is usually based on age (under thirty and over thirty, for example); although it can be based on method (lecture in one—discussion in the other), or it can be based on study materials used (Bible in one—application to social issues in the other). Obviously, the same results can be obtained by starting new classes for a younger group, or a discussion group, or a new type of study, encouraging those who wish to leave the present class and join others who are not in any class.

Under either method, feelings are very likely to be hurt and misunderstandings develop unless a lot of interpretation is done. The class and the church need to understand many of the principles outlined in this book (such as no class can stay young), and then those in charge need to move forward with courage.

Remember, God has in his wisdom made us very different persons and has never ordained or sanctified a particular size of group.

8.
Myth
Adults are essentially alike.

Reality
While adults share some common characteristics, recent research supports the desire and need for adults to be in groups of persons whose current state of life is much like theirs. Division by age focuses on the stages of life and the transitions from one to another, while the particular needs of young singles, or recently divorced adults, are met in many ways by classes just for them.

Grouping Adults

There has been one long-term basic shift in grouping adults over the last one hundred and fifty years: from age and sex to age and marital status.

In the 1800s and early 1900s most classes were for young

51

men or young women, and for older men and older women. There were a number of so-called "mixed" classes of men and women very early in the 1800s, but they were discouraged during the years between the Civil War and World War I. Right after World War I, in the 1920s, "young married couples'" classes sprang up everywhere, and those classes are just now—sixty years later—beginning to end their days with their members in their eighties. Thus, the first shift was from age and sex to age and married. The newest shift is to organize classes for both younger and older single adults, many of whom are divorced.

Why were most adult classes divided by sex—men's classes and women's classes? While I am not *sure* why this was true for most during the 1800s, I believe there were two primary reasons. First, it was believed that such groups had *more in common* than any other possible groupings. Men went to work and supported their families; women organized the home and cared for the children. Furthermore, men were thought to have definite and identifiable male characteristics, and women definite women characteristics, many of which we would not defend as true today. Furthermore, it was believed they "naturally" wanted to be together with their own sex.

Second, it was thought by some that to be so divided, the temptation to be "diverted from study" by the opposite sex would be lessened. Of course, early Christian groups in the Bible followed the pattern of the synagogue in which only the men took part and the women were separated by a screen beyond which they observed.

Some denominations, most notably the Southern Baptist, still hold up men's and women's classes as the officially most desirable, although there are *many* mixed classes, men and women together, in that church today.

"Development" in Adult Life

"Development" is an "in" word when thinking of adults in the 1970s and 1980s. The view that once an adult, always an adult, is gone, and in its place is a lot of research on the stages of adult life and some beginning work on the stages of faith development in adults.

Such ideas are far from entirely new, but today's theories are based on a great deal more detailed research than ever before. The Talmud, in the "Sayings of the Fathers," had a rather detailed understanding of "the ages of man," as did Shakespeare.

Our various curricula have paid considerable attention to the "Developmental Tasks" of Robert Havighurst and the "Persistent Life Concerns" of Erik Erikson. In twenty-five years of familiarity with the church's attempts to relate Christian learning to either of the above, I've become convinced that it is a mistake to take either theories or research of this kind and apply it directly to persons in the church.

Interestingly enough, a high percentage of the current research of persons like Levinson, *The Seasons of a Man's Life*, and Sheehy, *Passages, Predictable Crises of Adult Life*, is focused on persons on either the East or West Coasts of the United States. Few of the persons included in the research lived active church lives, and for most of them, neither religion nor the church played a decisive role. This is simply not true of the majority of people with whom we work in the Sunday school and the church in other parts of the country.

I hope that we will do a lot of thinking and work on the implications of this latest research, but I believe it is far too early to reach many conclusions. There are several ideas, though, which I feel have implications for adult Sunday school classes:

1. Adults need a lot of peer support as they go through the stable and transitional periods of their lives. The ongoing Sunday school class is ideally suited for this task, and I'm sure, can be strengthened in that role.

2. Ongoing classes, divided roughly by age, are substantially supported by such research. The trial and error method of learning to move successfully through a time such as the "Mid-Life Transition," is greatly aided by frequent conversation with others involved in the same process. At the same time, classes of older single persons

do much the same kind of thing for one another, as they survive divorces or deaths of their spouses and thread their way to a new type of life-style.

3. Levinson's discovery of the vital role of *mentor* is suggestive to me of the need young adults have for older persons as teachers and sponsors, as well as the encouragement and enablement of some *spiritual mentor* roles we Protestants have rarely developed.

I have not quoted at length from any of the books on adult development here, but they are listed in the bibliography, and I strongly suggest that those who are interested in the subject find and read several of them.

The idea that an adult goes through a pattern of "faith development," which includes definite *structures*, irrespective of the content of one's faith, is being carefully explored by Jim Fowler and his associates. His book, with Sam Keen, is entitled, *Life-Maps: Conversations on the Journey of Faith*. Fowler believes there are certain minimum ages at which a person may begin to move into another stage of faith development, but he has also found that many adults remain in a particular stage all their adult lives. A part of his hypothesis is that as far as Christian faith (or any other faith) is concerned, one stage of faith development is as good as any other. The stages do not go up in an ascending order, but have a consistent world view surrounding them which makes a "full-faith life" satisfying for that person.

This research gives me an explanation of a reality I have often observed. Some adults get very excited and stimulated by the personal discovery of a historical critical approach to the scriptures, and all of a sudden they say, "For the first time the Bible makes sense and has come alive for me." Other adults view such an approach with suspicion, and often open hostility, and sometimes say, "If I studied the Bible that way, it would undermine my faith, and I wouldn't know what to believe!"

According to Fowler, these two points of view illustrate two different stages of faith development (roughly his stages three and four) and show that some persons are ready to move from one stage to another, while others are not. Interesting unanswered questions are, What kinds of factors cause a person to want to move from one stage to another? and, What kind of roles can teachers and others play to facilitate that move?

For those of us who have observed the life of many adult Sunday school classes, it is obvious that some classes live very definitely within one particular stage of faith development, while another class is made up of persons in another structure of faith. Thus, a person may visit either one of these classes and decide not to return, saying, "That class does not satisfy my spiritual needs," or even, "I don't think those persons are even Christian! You should hear how they talk about the Bible!"

This book takes the position that through an informal process of self-selection, classes should be allowed to form around a particular stage of faith development, as long as the class does not become hostile toward other classes and the church as a whole.

When the social and support characteristics of the adult class are clearly understood and affirmed, allowing adults to group themselves on the basis of what *they* consider most helpful makes good sense. Adult classes are, of course, voluntary organizations to which adults are attracted, not forced, to attend.

Ideally, every church would be large enough, and diverse enough, to be able to give a wide choice to every adult. Of course, since the vast majority of churches have under two hundred members, this is not possible. In fact, it is usually a mistake for all churches to try to have every kind of class. This is well illustrated today by the great interest in classes for single persons. Recently, a person wrote to me saying his small church was going to try to have a singles' class, but it would have to include persons from eighteen to ninety. He asked what I thought about it. My answer was that persons eighteen to ninety have little in common, even if they are both single, and that it would be a mistake to try such a group. Persons at each end of that age span usually feel more at home with their own age group, even if all the rest are married. Quite possibly the eighteen-year-old should be urged to attend a nearby church where there are other young singles.

Two categories of adults are growing rapidly and will rapidly take the spotlight in our churches. They are single adults (for a variety of reasons), and senior adults (over sixty-five). We will give special attention to those two groups here.

The Sunday School and the Unmarried

The entire church and Sunday school are being forced to reexamine their ministry with those who are not married. The emphasis of the church for all of its history in the United States has been on the *family*—a married couple with children. This was the *norm*—all others were a little off the norm—especially in the small country church and the suburban church, where Protestant Sunday schools flourished.

Of course, there were widows, but they *had* been married. And, a few never married, but they *should*, or soon would, get married. Being married, contrary to Paul in I Corinthians, has been the "best" and "most desirable" state in the Protestant church.

Now—that is changing. The unmarried portion of the population is surging ahead. One out of three adults is single—in America there are approximately 43,000,000 adults (*Single Adults Want to Be the Church, Too* by Britton Wood).

There are many single persons who are *choosing* to remain single as a way of life. The increase in divorce, the national imbalance between men and women, and the increasing social acceptability of singleness are all factors.

There are *many* more divorced persons—some have had two or more marriages. Many are single parents, and a small number are single parents who have never been married.

The life span is lengthening, and as it does, a growing number of persons, usually women, are outliving their spouses by fifteen to twenty-five years.

There are churches today where single persons make up more than 50 percent of the congregation.

The married family is no longer the norm.

In the 1920s, when men's classes and women's classes went on a sharp decline, single persons stayed either in the remaining men's and women's classes or joined the couples' classes. In churches where *all* ongoing classes were abolished, singles, of course, were part of the subject-focused classes which were created. Such a move provided the single person with a "place" far better than other groupings.

Single Adult Classes Today

Young singles (usually under thirty) and older singles (usually thirty to fifty-five), and men's and women's classes (usually fifty-five to ninety) are the *major* patterns for singles' classes in the 1980s. Increasingly, where there are enough single persons to form a group, there is a desire for a singles' class; although in small towns often this is not considered desirable. "We marrieds and singles are together all the time, why be separated in Sunday school?" is a comment heard in smaller communities.

"Single-again" classes are appearing, and "Parents Without Partners" is another emphasis for singles with children.

A large number of books have been written in the last few years concerning the church's ministry with single adults. Most of the books written either in the Northeast or the Far West assume that young singles, especially, will be helped *only* by groups *other than* Sunday morning Sunday school classes. This is probably true in those regions, but certainly not true in the South or Midwest. Two books which suggest helpful approaches on either coast are by Dow and Brown and are listed in the bibliography.

The best book that I have found concerning single adult Sunday school classes is by Britton Wood and is entitled, *Single Adults Want to Be the Church, Too*. Mr. Wood directed a very large program for single adults at the Park Cities Baptist Church, in Dallas, Texas, for several years. Interestingly enough, this church is on the same street, only a couple of miles distant, as Lovers Lane United Methodist Church, which also has a large program for single adults, directed by Dick Schaefer.

These two churches illustrate quite well two successful approaches toward programming for singles, described by Mr. Wood in *Single Adults Want to Be the Church, Too*. At Lovers Lane a basic "Program-to-People Approach" is used, in which the leadership is brought in largely from the outside, and the classes are thus encouraged to grow quite large, with a variety lecture format. I often teach both the "Roaring Twenties" (about sixty in attendance), and the "Single Adults," most are over thirty years of age (over four hundred in attendance). They are exceedingly vital groups who draw persons from all over the city.

Down the street, Mr. Wood tried the "People-to-Program Approach," in which the single classes are kept relatively small (but *many* classes), and in which most of the programming originates from within the class. He believes that such an approach has slower, but more manageable, growth than the program-to-people style. I believe they are two very vital options.

My major observation in regard to classes for singles is that there must be enough prospects for a group to have a *mixture of men and women*, and there should not be too many persons who are emotionally, mentally, or physically handicapped. Many large groups of singles carry out an outstanding ministry with such members, but if "problem" people dominate the group, it will either turn overwhelmingly in that direction or die. This means that many small churches cannot start, or sustain, a class for singles, and should not try.

Also, a strong professional leader is *the key* to the strength of most large, urban programs for singles.

Better Than Geritol

Persons over sixty-five are a very rapidly growing portion of our population. A study done for the Department of Health,

Education and Welfare, showed that by the year two thousand, one out of every three Americans will be over sixty-five. Some people feel the study is exaggerated, but the fact is that this age group is one of the fastest growing segments of our population.

It is also one of the most controversial groups, with several of those controversies bearing directly on the adult Sunday school class. Most notable of these is the question of *segregation by age*. Some older adults find a group of persons their own age to be depressing, and even oppressive. Other persons the same age say they like to visit with younger people and be with them on occasion, but they really prefer to be in groups like themselves—especially in Sunday school.

While I find the latter group to be in the majority, it seems that certainly we need alternatives available wherever possible.

A few years ago I performed a wedding ceremony for a couple seventy and seventy-five years old. Their earlier spouses had been dead over a dozen years. We reflected on the Sunday school options for a couple like them and began to realize that nearly all persons their age went to either men's or women's classes. There were few classes for couples in their seventies and eighties! This is, in fact, another phenomenon of our time, as the age span lengthens and new marriages among the elderly become more and more common.

Erik Erikson in *Childhood and Society* has said that the principal challenge for older adults is "Ego Integrity vs. Despair." By integrity, I believe he meant the capacity to "bring things together" so that one can find integrity in one's existence, making some sense out of life, and thus continuing to "move ahead" with purpose and commitment. Despair, on the other hand, is sitting down and becoming a burden to oneself and to others, stagnating.

Certainly this same challenge faces adult classes of older persons. The temptation to look back to the golden age of that class, when attendance was high, service projects were great, and the members were "in their prime" is very great.

Actually, as is also discussed in section two, each class of

59

older persons has a unique ministry to perform for and to persons like themselves, as well as having opportunities to be elders in the midst of groups of children or teen-agers. In a society where families so often live hundreds of miles from grandparents, surrogate grandparents can be a real gift for those growing up.

In the next ten to twenty years, several new approaches and many new classes of persons over sixty-five will need to be organized. This will be one of the largest avenues of service for which the adult Sunday school class is ideally suited.

9.

Myth
All adult classes need common *goals and practices.*

Reality
One of the greatest strengths of adult classes is particular commitments to particular causes in which members identify themselves. A real sense of "we"ness helps a class have enthusiasm and energy to carry out its perceived mission.

While such enthusiasm can become extremely self-centered, and even sectarian in some instances, too much conformity usually results in loss of personal investment and power.

Where Is the Energy of the Church?

Every church has energy to get things done and to accomplish its goals. Much, if not most, of that energy is found in the enthusiastic small groups of the church. Such groups as the choir, the women's organization, or an ongoing adult Sunday school class give evidence of much energy and enthusiasm. In many ways, these groups could be called "sects" within the body of the church.

They exhibit their sectarian enthusiasm by their sense of "we"ness against the "they"ness of the other organizations and persons in the church. Many persons in these groups develop a fierce loyalty to their group, and they feel that everyone (or nearly everyone) should be a part of their group.

Such enthusiasm and sense of belonging can, of course, be both positive and negative. *But*, a church will have little energy without such groups, and more groups will usually produce more energy. This is true of most groups in a church, but here we are interested in adult Sunday school classes.

Fifteen to twenty years ago several denominations focused their attention on the limitation of ongoing adult classes in which persons stayed for most of their adult lives. These denominations urged churches to abandon such groups and organize, instead, a series of adult classes that would focus on the content of study. Such groups would be reorganized every three months, or so, and people would reenroll in another group focused on another topic with another leader.

The short-term, rotating groups, by and large, take their lesson materials more seriously than many ongoing classes. Nevertheless, they usually fail to develop the *energy* of ongoing classes, except in the area of study. They do not develop the long-term attitude of caring/sharing as do long-term classes, nor do they produce the support for the church as an organization as do ongoing classes.

It is a basic truth that when new ongoing adult Sunday school classes, which meet a real need, are started, the energy in the church is increased. More service projects will be undertaken, more enthusiastic evangelistic contacts will be made, and more persons will identify with a group in which they feel supported as a person.

Interestingly enough, a church often needs more new classes of the type it already has, rather than classes for

61

persons who are not presently in the Sunday school. For instance, it is a mistake to believe that *every* church needs a class for single young adults. In fact, many smaller churches are doing a disservice to both the church and the young singles by trying to hold together a very small class when a few miles away another church has a much stronger class which exhibits most of the desirable characteristics of an ideal class for young single adults.

If we are really primarily interested in the spiritual welfare of individuals, we must set aside our desire to have our church serve the needs of every kind of person and urge our young single adults to go to that nearby vital group. In Denver and a few other cities, several churches in a particular part of the city have formed such a class together, sometimes denominationally and occasionally ecumenically.

On the positive side, the church that already has two classes of adults whose age range is about forty to sixty may very well need one or two more classes for this age group. But the members of the existing classes are likely to be the most articulate opponents of starting new classes for "our prospects."

It is important, but often not easy, to help such classes see the sociological realities of their own class. Let me list a few I have found to be usually true:

1. Most adult classes reach their maximum size within a year after they start. While I could list several exceptions to this statement (a singles group in Dallas, four years old, suddenly jumped from forty to two hundred in the space of a year) this is a rare exception. The establishment of warm, primary friendships, the type of teaching method usually used, and the original enthusiasm of the charter group all contribute to this leveling-off process.

2. Persons who once belonged to such classes but are now inactive *rarely* return to their old class but may find a new class attractive. The clash of personalities, the uneven spiritual growth of individuals, and the changing interests and needs of persons (such as a divorce) all contribute to this reality.

3. Often newcomers to the church, who have visited the

two existing classes but have not joined, would rather be a part of a new group where they may share in the leadership than to "fight their way in" which they feel they would have to do in the present groups.

When carefully conducted surveys reveal substantial numbers of persons of a particular age group (say forty to sixty) not active in the existing classes, and when several persons who are approached directly show real interest, it is time to start a new class after working carefully with existing classes to interpret the need.

One of the major desires of *all* members of the church is more *energy* for the church as an organization and for the service of God through Christ.

10.
Myth
Class time around the coffeepot is wasted.

Reality
Much of the most important learning adults do is through informal conversation with respected peers in the process of modifying one's thinking and behavior in order to cope and survive. The time before and after the lesson is crucial for many in this regard.

"All That Wasted Time"

A whole cluster of other myths gathers around this one.
"The time the class takes to talk, and make plans, and celebrate birthdays and anniversaries is silly and wasted."

63

"If we took the full hour to study our lesson then we would learn more."

"When you take time for fellowship and class business, there is insufficient time for an adequate lesson."

"Because of the time around the coffeepot, the teacher is never able to *cover the lesson*."

While there is some truth in several of these statements, and while drinking coffee is not all that good for your health, time spent in informal conversation in a group of this kind is rarely wasted. Adult learning is discussed further in myth fourteen so I will limit my comments here to the nature of informal learning.

We should never equate learning with "lessons." Adults learn all the time, in many ways, one of which may be from a "lesson."

Learning for Surviving

When it comes right down to it, the only thing a man or woman *has* to learn is to survive. Self-preservation, closely tied to the protection of those we love, is a commandment built into our very being. There *are* causes for which we will sacrifice our lives, as well as persons for whom we will die, but our basic drive in life is to *live* and to make sense out of that living. That is what often happens around the coffeepot.

For most people, the fortitude for life does not come from ideas, in and of themselves, but comes instead from people. When God wanted to give us a gift that would give us life, he gave us a life, a person—his Son. God also gave us each other, and we need to share with others our problems and our joys.

Several years ago my wife and I frequently attended a couples' class of persons who were generally between forty and fifty-five years of age. All our children were teen-agers, and the years were the early 1970s.

After getting a cup of coffee, I usually joined a group of four or five men. The conversation often included the football games of the day before, or the "big" game coming up that afternoon. The other major topic was children. The conversation might begin,

"Do you know what my daughter said she wanted to do this past week?" Of course, we said, "No." "Sometimes my wife and I simply don't know what we are going to do!"

Sometimes there was nearly an embarrassed silence, because it was obvious that for this man and his wife their problem was crucial. Then, slowly, several of the men would speak. At first the words were primarily sympathetic, and then sometimes someone would say, "That isn't anything compared to what my son did!" A few minutes later another person might say, "Well, I don't know whether it will help or not, but when that same thing happened to us, my wife and I decided that we simply had to ————." The first man would then question the last speaker and would probe the reasons for his decision, and possibly ask, "How did you get your wife to go along?" Others of us might, or might not, enter into the dialogue, but you can be sure we were filing away in our heads the conversation we were hearing, and on many Sundays I would tell my wife about the conversation on the way home from church. Now this is *real* learning, most valuable learning, and it will rarely be learned from a lesson.

You may be saying, "But his story was horrible, and he was given very poor advice. If they had only heard the 'expert' I heard the other night, they would be so much better off!" But, true or false as this may be, it is in the trusting one-to-one relationship where I feel I can *really* be helped with a problem like mine. Of course, such a problem is so personal and so powerful that the man would never raise it in the entire class. He would feel much too exposed, and his wife might hit him with her purse!

A long-time teacher of one adult class says that not infrequently a few persons in the class will talk with him after class about something he said in the session. Usually they will say, "I didn't want to bring it up before the whole class, but I'd sure like to hear you say more about ————."

At other times, as he is standing around before the class starts, a person will come up and say, "You know, Howard, I've been worrying over something we talked about in class three weeks ago, and I simply can't get it out of my mind!"

Here is deep reflective learning, waiting for more data before continuing its pondering.

This same teacher says that frequently a person will say, "Have you heard that Bill and Edith are having trouble?" or, "Did you know that Betty's son has had to go back to the hospital?" and immediately the members of the class who are standing around will begin to make plans to try to help in each situation.

Yes, often there is inadequate time for the formal lesson, but wasted time—hardly! It is crucial time for life and for death.

11.
Myth
*Adult classes are stronger
with few social events.*

Reality
Frequent social events and involvement in one or two significant service projects are two of the most significant aspects in the life of a strong class.

There *are* some ongoing classes (usually quite small) which do not want any activities at all except for the study they do together on Sunday morning. Such groups usually see one another only in the class and are persons who find most of their social life in other groups. Some of the persons in these groups are quite shy, have few friends, and little social contacts at all. My experience would indicate that such persons are quite satisfied and should not be urged to change their class. The same thing applies to most short-term, or elective, classes which study a subject for a period of weeks and then disband.

But

Most successful ongoing Sunday school classes are more than just a group of people who want to study the faith together. Research has shown that in many classes a significant percentage of the member's best personal friends are also members of that class (*The Parish Paper*, Yokefellow Institute, March 1974, Lyle E. Schaller, ed.). In fact, for many it was in the class where they first met, and it is through the life of the class that their friendships ripen into lasting bonds.

I recently visited a class in a Disciples of Christ church which exhibited such friendship to a very high degree. I happened to sit next to a man in his sixties who cordially introduced himself. After a brief conversation, he said he was Jewish—married to a member of this church. He said many years ago he started attending the class parties with his wife, and for several years he has faithfully attended the class itself. He continued, "These people are some of my best friends . . . I don't know what my life would be without them." Soon I realized that the same was true of a high percent of others in that class. Many of them were together two to three times a week—these were their best friends.

Interestingly enough, the very warmth of the personal ties of those in such a class often make it difficult to incorporate new people into that friendly community. Nearly all classes will insist they *want* to welcome newcomers and to make them feel a total part of the class, but this is difficult to practice without care and planning. There is, in fact, a psychological wall around such a group—invisible for those inside the group but very solid for many outside the group. This problem is analyzed in detail in chapter four, "The Dynamics of Inclusion and Exclusion," in *Assimilating New Members*, by Lyle E. Schaller.

Awareness of the reality, genuine desire to continually challenge it, and organizing in a way to assure openness are all important.

The seemingly insignificant matter of name tags is sometimes a key to this effort. When *everyone* wears name tags (not just the visitors or newcomers), all are on an equal footing, and a sharp memory is not essential to address a person by name.

The Importance of "Breaking Bread"

A common meal, from the symbolism of the Communion Service or the Love Feast of bread and water, to a "dinner on the grounds" has always been important in the church. In small churches which have only one adult class, it is usually the entire church which has "family basket dinners" or "potluck suppers."

In larger churches, some sort of eating together by adult classes is usually important. Writing in 1974 on "Ten Common Characteristics of Meaningful Adult Classes," Lyle E. Schaller says that one of these is class members eating together several times during the year. "This may be the monthly social event, it may be an occasional covered dish or carry in dinner, it may be picnics or other outings, or it may be only coffee and rolls every Sunday before class convenes. Not infrequently it is a combination of several of these" (*The Parish Paper*, Yokefellow Institute, March 1974, Lyle E. Schaller, ed.).

One very strong adult class in the Midwest had in its yearbook a firm policy: "Social meetings—Third Friday night of the month at 6:30 with a covered dish dinner, unless otherwise specified. Fellowship Hall has been reserved for these meetings" (The Brownie Sunday School Class Yearbook, 1972-73, Des Moines, Iowa). This was kept up for over fifty years, and now that the class has discontinued meeting on Sunday morning, occasional social events continue. Most members are now in their eighties.

An interesting variation on the eating-together patterns is an adult "Sunday School Class" which meets every week on a week night for both dinner and a lesson. My wife and I occasionally attend such a class in Dallas and find both the fellowship and lessons stimulating.

The Gift and the Giver

As I stepped into the small classroom of middle-aged men at a large Southern Baptist Church, the first thing that caught my attention was a number of snapshots of a young woman and a young man. Grouped together in a frame, the poses showed each person as a child, a teen-ager, and a high school graduate. Noticing my interest, one of the members told me that the class had "sponsored" these two young people for over fifteen years. Coming from broken homes as children, these young people had been literally "raised" by the men in this class. Many thousands of dollars had been given, also many loving and carefully chosen gifts, as well as several trips and visits to camps. Now they were both in college and were still being helped. Love, personal pride, sense of worthwhile achievement shone in the eyes of the man speaking to me.

One of the greatest problems in modern society is the bureaucratic separation of the gift and the giver. Nowhere is this truer than in the churches with a totally unified budget in which no group ever is allowed to give to specified projects or persons directly, but must always give through the church budget.

In my recent survey of over four hundred local churches across the country, only a small percentage had such a totally unified budget. The vast majority allowed their adult classes to use a portion of the money they raised to support projects of their own choosing. Many of these projects were not the kind that pleased the pastor or the officials of the church, and there were frequent efforts to guide the projects of adult classes into more direct denominational channels.

Nonetheless, there is widespread support for the great benefits in a class's long-term interest and care of persons or projects with which their members regularly and personally

69

identify. Support of this idea, as an important quality of a strong adult class, is given by Schaller and others (*The Parish Papers*, Yokefellow Institute, March 1974, Lyle E. Schaller, ed.).

Going back through many old books on adult classes, I have found lists of hundreds of such projects since the 1950s. Projects which do the most for a class are usually those that involve more than a *one-time* gift of money; they are long-term plans of support in which persons can work directly and can see the results of their labors over the years. Such things as: repairing toys through the year for gifts to hundreds of children at Christmas; opening, remodeling, and teaching in an outpost or mission Sunday school a few blocks, or miles, from the church; tutoring disadvantaged children on week nights to help them catch up with their peers in basic learning skills.

While most such projects fade in time, and many of them seem to make little overall impact on our society, there is no doubt at all of their value to the persons and groups who do them. Everyone wants her/his life to count for something, and I have watched many persons regain their sense of worth as they worked with others on such endeavors.

Most adult Sunday school classes need social events which are fun and service projects which are significant.

12.
Myth
*Adults are no longer motivated
to teach adult classes.*

Reality
*Our patterns of recruitment and training must
change radically. Recruitment must be for much
shorter periods of time (one month to three*

months) and must adapt itself to the realities of busy schedules. Today's adults do not want to be inadequate leaders and will respond to focused, quality training if they can be assured it will not be a waste of time. Candor—"telling the truth"—*is a vital key in both recruitment and training. Church persons expect to be lied to in this regard.*

Motivation: Has It Changed?

Yes. Motivation for "loyalty" reasons or "I ought" reasons has greatly decreased. Motivation for "doing a good job," for "accomplishing something worthwhile" and "because I enjoy the preparation" or "I enjoy the group very much" have taken over for many. These new motivations need to be recognized in both recruitment and training of teachers of adults.

I have spent twenty-five years holding hundreds of seminars, workshops, and labs for teachers of adults throughout the United States. These events varied from one or two hours to a full week in length. At times I traveled five hundred miles for a two-day workshop and only five persons came when thirty were expected. At other times, twenty were expected and twenty were there throughout the entire time. What makes the difference?

Were the persons in the latter workshop more Christian? I hardly think so. While there is always a complexity of factors, a pattern has emerged which I have identified over and over.

1. *Realism* in regard to schedule and time. Far too often a minister, or a small group who are not teachers plan the schedule for those they want to attract without consulting them.
2. Publicity about the event is largely limited to letters, announcements, and news articles, though everyone hears about it, no one is *committed to attend.* "Eyeball to

71

eyeball" contacts, or personal telephone calls, which ask for a specific commitment—not a "maybe I'll get by"—are essential.

3. General information on what will happen and who will lead will not attract many today. *Explicit, focused* content designed to meet felt-needs and direct information concerning the leader (not too much blarney) is also important.

4. The *endorsement* and *presence* of the pastor is often a key to success. I have often been in a large church for a workshop in which the entire event was obviously second-class. Most of the congregation did not even know it was going on, and the pastor showed no interest publicly or privately.

In my mind, all of these factors in recruitment for training are directly related to the new motivation. Twenty-five years ago many teachers came to such events because they were told *they should*. Today's motivation wants *candor* (the truth) and *realism* assured before making a commitment.

Are adults no longer motivated? No, only motivated in a different way.

Teacher Recruitment

Our survey of adult classes in four hundred churches this year reveals that about half of the existing adult classes have only one teacher and slightly over half have two or more teachers. Older classes tend to have one; younger classes tend to have more.

This data needs to be considered along with that of a survey made a few years ago in The United Methodist Church which showed that one of the major reasons adults in that denomination attend a class is their liking of and trust in the teacher.

A third factor in teacher recruitment today is the mobility of the population, both frequent moving from one community to another and the commitment to non-church activities on many weekends.

This leads me to another myth of the Sunday school: it is important to consider what we do each Sunday as a part of a continuum in both curriculum writing and teaching. In point of fact, especially in classes of young marrieds and singles, attendance is extremely irregular (there is nearly a "new" class each Sunday), and so to be effective each Sunday's lesson must "stand on its own feet," depending little on either the Sunday before or after.

A final finding of our survey is information concerning teaching methods used in adult classes. About one-third of the classes hear *only* lectures (most with one teacher), less than one-third have discussion only, the largest number combine some form of lecture and discussion each Sunday. The majority of these latter classes are younger, newer, and have more than one teacher.

What do these factors tell us about motivation and recruitment of teachers of adults?

1. In today's world, we need to recruit teachers on the basis of *realism*—without too much pretension, based on proven educational theory. Specifically, this means recruiting teachers for a wide variety of periods of time—from every Sunday for a year, to one Sunday a month, or possibly a two-month period once a year. While this *will* decrease loyalty in many classes to one highly respected teacher, it will also allow the church to "use" many excellent people for the times they are willing or able to give.

2. We also need to recruit teachers on the basis of methods they are willing and able to use. While there are many methods used in adult classes, the three primary ones are clear: lecture, discussion, or lecture and discussion. Though we need persons able to do all three, in most churches we need persons who are willing to lecture *and* lead discussion. As discussed in detail in myths fifteen and sixteen, a "better/worse" rating has been imposed on this list in the past, which I and others are challenging.

When an outstanding lady says, "I am quite able to prepare a good lecture, but I always 'flop' when trying to lead a discussion," we need to take her at her word and recruit her on that basis. When another person—possibly a young executive—responds, "I could never pull off a lecture—especially a long one—but I sure can keep a group talking," we need to believe it. While both of these persons may try a few other things later, the strong likelihood is that their basic style will remain the same.

3. Recruitment of teachers of adults today can also be on the basis of curriculum. This was taught to me the first time about twenty years ago when one of our excellent teachers said, "I'm a little tired of teaching the same class, and I've prepared a six-week course on 'The Christian Faith and Communism.' How about telling other classes I'm available for six-week periods to teach that course?" Over a period of years Harry taught that course to a number of classes, and I'm sure he got better as he went along.

"Sally, didn't you teach a course on 'World Hunger and Christian Life-Styles' to your women's group a year ago? Why not let us announce that you will be available to adult classes to do the same course in a four-week period?"

It is tragic that so many fine studies are prepared for groups other than Sunday school, taught once, and never heard from again. Why should a woman not become an "expert" on the Gospel According to Luke and teach it to several classes and youth groups?

Many ministers let it be known that they are available to teach a certain course to youth and adult classes, and various classes invite them to do so.

Time span, method, and course of study are three bases on which teachers of adult classes may be recruited. Many churches have a sort of "teacher pool" from which they may draw as the need arises. I have found this may be a pool of five persons in a small church to a pool of fifty to seventy-five in a very large church. While *most* teachers will probably be recruited directly by a class on the basis of, "We would like you to be one of our three regular teachers," building up an available group has also proved quite beneficial.

There is no doubt what is most desirable in a teacher of adults. It is *a mature and growing faith and commitment to the God we know in Jesus Christ.* Biblical knowledge helps, a winning personality is great, skills in teaching are an asset, but *a faith to share* is what we need the most!

Many are still around who have such faith and are willing and able—but we need to use realism in inviting them to teach.

Education and Training for Teachers of Adults

One of my favorite books is by Philip Anderson and is entitled, *Church Meetings That Matter.* Never mind what's in the book (it *is* very useful), isn't that a wonderful title? Haven't you been to many, many church meetings—including training for teachers—that didn't matter? That were, in fact, a terrible waste of time.

I believe that is one of the primary reasons we have trouble getting people to go to training events. We are less than candid when we assure them (without knowing), "It will be a fine school, and your teacher will be very good!" The final product often cannot be compared to the sales pitch!

How can we have educational and training events for teachers of adults that will matter?

Teachers of adult Sunday school classes are, by and large, busy people. They are the persons who accept responsibility in several organizations and are anxious to do a good job in each. They often are overextended. Consequently, most teachers of adult classes do not attend "any old training that might help a little." They are more selective, and often harder to persuade, than teachers of children and youth. By and large, they are older, they have been to more events, and they are more skeptical of the possibilities.

In addition, for the last twenty years, *many* of the denominationally sponsored events for teachers of adults have stressed *radical change* in both method and content. They have consistently attacked the use of lecture and the use of the Uniform Lesson Series—both of which are used by the majority of adult classes. They have urged (with very little success) the use of films, tapes, and other teaching methods which require mechanical devices for their use. Many churches do not have such equipment—most teachers do not feel comfortable with it, and it is used only marginally. Such training events have often made group discussion into a semigod (see myths fifteen and sixteen) instead of a useful teaching tool.

Trust is one of the key factors in motivation, and many teachers of adults do not trust those who organize the training. I have learned over the years to *expect* those who want me to go to something to be overly enthusiastic, and often to hide from me part of the realities. (This leader was not our first choice but the only one we could get at the last minute is seldom admitted.)

The churches, by and large, have failed in their chain of leadership. Persons on a national level train those on a regional level, who in turn train those on a local level. The trust level drops drastically toward the end of the chain, with the exception of laboratory leaders (trained in depth), and some leaders in the women's organization. Adults want to believe that the leader knows more than they do—they are looking for *quality* and competence. If they believe it will be there, they will often come.

What We Need

1. *Bible Study*

Above all else, teachers of adults want to know more *about* the Bible and want to be able to lead their classes *into* the Bible. They need to know how to use Bible helps (concordance, atlas, commentary) and they need to *experience* methods of Bible study.

Usually, the pastor of the church, or another seminary-trained person, is the most likely instructor. Small churches often get together for this study.

Times and frequency of meeting and the length of a study

are *very* important. (Four two-hour periods on Sunday afternoon—three one and one-half hour periods on Wednesday—one all-day Saturday workshop (9:00 A.M. to 3:30 P.M.) are all possibilities. What is *essential*, is that the planners have commitments from the participants *before* they try the training. The plans that work will differ greatly in different communities.

2. *Lesson Preparation and Use of Curriculum Material*

A new teacher of adults, of course, needs this *first*—before starting to teach, if possible.

A very successful pattern for this kind of training is a "Demonstration Weekend Clinic," in which a leader spends three hours on Saturday with a group preparing a lesson, teaches it to one of their classes on Sunday morning, with all of them attending the demonstration while substitutes teach their classes, and evaluates the experience after church for two hours on Sunday afternoon.

3. *Workshops on Teaching Methods*

The heart of these should be on "Improving the Lecture" and "Conducting Discussions," with the introduction of other methods very secondary.

These events should be sharply *focused* (as "Improving Your Lectures" or "Lecture Outline") and can be held on one evening (two and one-half hours), or on a Saturday morning.

4. *Christian Beliefs, Church History, Ethics, World Religions*

Education is a broadening process in which a person becomes aware of other perspectives and reflects upon their implications. Much of the religious education of the teacher of adults will come through individual reading and, on occasion, courses at colleges or universities. Nevertheless, local churches, groups of churches, and larger church bodies can offer the teacher high quality experiences in these areas also.

Teachers of adults *will* take part in high quality education and training.

13.
Myth
*Adult teachers who become "stars"
are liabilities.*

Reality

*While in some instances adult teachers have
developed cults around themselves which have
led persons away from the church, many greatly
beloved teachers are inspiring models for their
class.*

*We have gone through an anti-hero period in
recent years, sometimes believing that a "team"
is always better than one outstanding person.
Phillips Brooks said, "Preaching is truth
through personality." This is true of great
teaching as well.*

In the Teaching/Learning Equation the Teacher Is 90 Percent

"Our teacher loves and is concerned about all of us."

"My teacher both teaches and lives her faith."

"When I'm not sure about the lesson writers I *know* I can trust our teacher."

"Some of our teachers are more helpful than others, but each one is very sincere."

In our pursuit of life we do not follow ideas—we follow people. When God wanted to fully reveal himself he came *in a person,* and we know God through that person (Jesus Christ) and many other persons. *Personality is an asset, not a liability.* But that means we often give more worth to a person than we should. That is the risk we always take with a strong, winsome, attractive person.

Many people "join a minister" rather than join a church. The same is true in many Sunday school classes. The longer I live, the more I am certain that I want to go where I am confident the leader has something to give to me—if I have a choice.

Be an S. R. O.

Sociologists have spoken of "significant others" for many years, and recently I have found it useful to add a middle word, *respected*. Everyone of us is potentially a "significant, respected other" for somebody, but this is especially true of the trusted and loved Sunday school teacher. Many adults have few *really close* friends other than their husbands or wives, and all of us need a few S. R. O.'s. These are persons whose view of us is very important to us, whom we respect, and who are distant enough from us not to be a threat.

The teacher of an adult class has the advantage of working week after week at a significant religious issue in our presence and in dialogue with us. This means that that person "exposes" his/her thoughts, feelings, faith, and doubts in a way that makes it possible for many of us to do the same. We often want the approval and respect of such persons, and when they urge us to self-examination, we are likely to pay attention. *Yes, the trusted teacher of adults is an S. R. O. for many.*

One Teacher or More?

If the teacher is *really* so important, do we dare have several instead of one? Increasingly adult classes *do* have several teachers on rotation system, partly because that is the basis on which they can get them, but also because many classes prefer a variety of personalities instead of one.

My observation is that the more teachers an adult class has, the less the members are going to closely identify with one, but that does not mean that close relationships do not develop. When a member of a large church staff, I was always reminded that some members of the church found one of the ministers much more helpful and trustworthy (for them) than the others. This is also true of several teachers of adults, and the different teachers enrich the variety of the class. Each teacher may "star" in his or her own way!

Recently, one of my students surveyed a number of ministers in Northern Louisiana, asking what were the most important factors in adult class success. By far the largest number replied, "The teacher," followed by "the fellowship of the class."

Curriculum materials have some value, the room in which the class meets and the make-up of the class are important, but overwhelmingly it is *the teacher* or *teachers* who make the crucial difference.

III.
Myths and Realities
on Teaching/Learning

14.
Myth
Adults learn what they are taught.

Reality
Adults are very much in charge of their own learning. Adults have developed very strong bunk detectors by which they turn on and off their attention, a procedure which enables them to pick and choose what they consider valid.

Adults are most motivated to learn at points where they have problems to solve or where they are experiencing anxiety or pain.

Teachers should accept the ways in which adults learn and not try to "take it over." Teachers should plan their lessons to engage the class at "entrance points" to the lesson and should encourage class members to think beyond the lesson itself.

Adult Learning Versus Adult Education

Adult *learning* and adult *education* must always be distinguished. Adults *are learning all the time* through casual conversation, through watching and listening, through reading and thinking on their own. Occasionally an adult enrolls in an adult education course, or goes regularly to an adult Sunday school class, but those are only a small part of adult learning.

This is especially true in learning the Christian faith and the implication for living that faith in daily life. A woman and her husband of many years do much of their Christian learning as they talk hour after hour about how they should deal with their children, or how they can best care for their aged parents, or how they can live together over the coming years and fulfill the needs and aspirations of each other. Bringing their faith, their thoughts, their experiences, and their reaction to the daily news into conversation with each other, the couple develops strategies and plans in which they experiment with their learning.

What every teacher of an adult class needs to remember is that when the couple arrives at Sunday school that ongoing learning process is in full swing and is actually interrupted by the lesson. As is worked out in myth eighteen, the lesson is not unimportant in the total learning environment because it brings into the minds of the adults an outside element, a series of scriptural experiences quite different from the daily experiences of the persons in the class, and this broadens the perspective of the learner and forces the individual adult to consider additional options.

Adults and Change

Many adults have listened to countless sermons and have taken part in several Sunday school lessons, all of which have stressed the Christian attitude toward persons of other races, and yet those adults seem to be as prejudiced as ever. Do adults actually learn? If so, how?

I no longer remember the source of the story of a man who lived in a two-story house with a dog. Every night when he went upstairs to bed the dog would curl up on the landing to sleep. Each morning, groping his way downstairs seeking his coffee, the man got to the landing, tripped on the dog, and fell the rest of the way down the stairs! Telling his friends about it, this adult always said, "You would think after all these months that dumb dog would learn better!"

So it seems, indeed, with many adults—they often expect the *other* person to learn and to change, not themselves. Actually, of course, adults learn a great deal, but often not in the areas where others of us wish they would. Wives and husbands are very familiar with this reality as they struggle over the years to get the other to change into the person they "ought" to be. "If only she would listen to me!"

Today, millions of adults are engaged in some form of formal adult or continuing education, a large percentage of whom attend adult Sunday school classes. While some adults are working for college degrees, most adults attend informal classes which they enjoy and in which they learn. Many of these classes are chosen by adults who think they want to learn that material, but even more are courses related directly to the adult's work, and the employee is often required, or strongly urged, to attend. In many of these cases, the employee is *paid* to attend the class, the company believing that it is worth the cost.

But, far more important for adult learning than classes on

one subject or another, are all the self-initiated learning projects that adults do on their own. A man wants a boat which he cannot afford; so he buys a kit and *learns* how to build it himself. A couple wants a vacation cottage; so they *learn* together how to do nearly everything to build it. A woman wants to improve her job potential; so she takes a self-directed course in accounting or business management.

Adults Learn

Adults are motivated to learn when they feel a need. That need may be an interior curiosity or an external promise of a raise, but it is motivating to that person. In the area of the Christian faith the need may be felt as a desire to do better with a fifteen-year-old son or to understand why the church wants me to have my child baptized. It may be the need to talk more intelligently about your denomination to the man who works next to you, or to grow in your feeling of knowing God for your own spiritual enrichment.

We know several things about adult learning.

1. Adult learning often involves a good deal of unlearning, because the new information is contrary to one's past experiences and knowledge. It is not easy to unlearn and it often takes many months or years.

2. Adults direct their own learning. They do not simply learn what they hear—otherwise they would be inundated with a virtual flood of information from TV and many other sources. I like to say that adults develop built-in *bunk* detectors, which allow them to turn off in their minds much of what they hear. They simply think *bunk* and dismiss the data as being false or inconsequential.

3. Adults learn through their past experiences. Adults have had a multitude of experiences, and often when they are told something they simply think to themselves, "Yes, that fits my experience," or "That is nonsense. I have had different experiences."

4. Adults must be engaged to learn. This principle is often

misunderstood. It does not mean that the learner has to do much, or any, talking to be engaged. It only means that his/her mind must be engaged with the ideas and the experiences.

5. Adults learn in light of their responsibilities and relationships. This is of critical importance in understanding adult learning. I can hardly learn something which will cause me to lose my job, or which will jeopardize my marriage, or which will lead me to change my responsibility to my children. At least, I will have to have *very* strong motivation to do so.

6. Adults *fit* their learning into the culture and context of which they are a part. This sometimes so changes the learning that the person on the outside thinks that the adult has "corrupted" the idea so badly that it is no longer the same. Whether that is true or not, an adult has not really learned something until he/she has brought it fully into his/her world.

Thus, when adults learn they do not restrict their learning to the data which is *presented* to them. This has *always* been true when Christians learn the Christian faith. They always learn it (the lesson, for instance) by bringing it into conversation with the culture of which they are a part—of the time in which they live—and with the necessities of their own lives (such as keeping reasonable peace with their mother). This has often been called "selective perception."

Many scholars of religion in modern America are very critical of this phenomenon when it occurs in the adult Sunday school class. Nevertheless, all important adult learning (learning for survival) is done in this fashion, and if the faith is *not* "corrupted" in the process it is obviously not learned. Real adult learning *must* assimilate and contaminate the data it receives, or it cannot make the new data part of its existence.

To say this, and to believe it, certainly does not mean that the educator simply surrenders to it. In The United Methodist Church in recent years we have said that our theological thinking should be based on what is called the "Wesley quadrilateral": Scripture, tradition, experience, and reason.

This simply means that we try to introduce evidence from each of these sources to test the others as we attempt to understand the implications of the faith for daily decisions.

Forced exposure to data and experiences not commonly a part of one's daily fare is surely a key to *education*. This is one of the primary functions of curriculum resources. But such *exposure* is never to be equated with acceptance of what one has been exposed to.

How do *you actually* learn and grow as an adult? How do you continue your education? Recently, I asked a colleague of mine these questions, and after a moment's reflection he said, "That's easy—I simply agree to lead groups on subjects which are on the *edge* of my expertise." Isn't that an interesting response! What he meant was he accepted the challenge of stretching his knowledge and ability, knowing that in preparing to lead a group *he would have to learn*.

The same has certainly been true for me. I need a "built-in necessity" (agreeing to teach an adult class) to force me to push the limits of my present knowledge as I prepare to lead the thinking of others.

How Should We Teach Adults?

If the things that have been said here are true of adult learning, how should we teach adults? Myths fifteen, sixteen, and seventeen will deal with this question in their own way. It will be introduced here.

One of the great adult educators of the airlines industry, Mr. T. Lee, was well-known for the statement with which he started his classes, "Nobody ever taught nobody nothing."

His emphasis, of course, was on the fact that every adult is in charge of his/her own learning and that the skills or techniques of the teacher can rarely overcome the lack of motivation in the learner—especially in the adult.

I believe a lot of nonsense has been written in church circles concerning the teaching of adults; much of it attempts to apply directly certain popular theories concerning teaching adults secular subjects.

Therefore, it is most helpful for me to draw a rather sharp line between adult learning and teaching adults and to assume that while they hopefully overlap, they are never identical.

No adult ever learns precisely what she/he is taught. It is always filtered through the individual's personal thought processes and emotional commitments of each person.

How then, do we teach adults? For me there are four key elements: (1) a piece of data or experience, (2) engagement in some reflective way, (3) use of Christian criteria which allows meaning or purposefulness to emerge, and (4) the process.

All are important and have a variety of interesting facets.

I. *The data* (a story, information, idea, experience, a picture or painting, an object). Most adult Sunday school classes try to handle *too* much data, *too* fast, in a *too* superficial way. One reason for this is the amount of material found in the denominational curriulum resource book for that Sunday (usually six to eight pages), with the implication that it is all to be "covered" that Sunday, so the class can "go on" to the new material designed for the next week.

The adult teacher should *never use* such material (in its entirety) but should always *select* certain portions and focus the interest of the class on a few ideas with which they may possibly become involved, or engaged.

The idea that Sunday school class members will remember or benefit from a fast recital, or reading, of a wide variety of ideas, scripture quotations, or even a commentary on a long story in the Bible is rarely confirmed by actual experience.

Data carefully selected (either by the teacher, or by the participants as the class goes along) and then explored, reflected upon, stories told about and applications suggested will provide a far more interesting and beneficial experience than a wide survey.

II. *Engagement.* In most states it is against the law to drive a car in neutral (even coasting downhill), because the engagement of the gears helps the driver maintain control, as well as enabling the car to get somewhere.

In a similar fashion, material that just coasts by and never engages the participants is seldom remembered or used.

Unfortunately, much has been written in adult education on the assumption that involvement, or engagement, with ideas requires articulation on the part of the participants and that the more said the higher the level of involvement.

Exactly the opposite may be true. Some adults talk (often a lot) to keep from getting too involved with key ideas; while other adults engage the ideas brought up in serious, but silent, conversation within their own minds.

A very good lecturer, who uses a form of "dialogical-monologue" can often succeed in significant engagement and involvement of hundreds of persons with the material he/she is exploring in their presence, without anyone in the audience saying a word at all.

I was a student of Reinhold Niebuhr in seminary some thirty years ago. His classes were usually large. Often there was no discussion or questions by anyone in an entire hour, and yet, I rarely left his classroom uninvolved. In fact, I was usually *so* engaged with his ideas that it would take two or three hours of debriefing with a couple of other students before I could calm down.

III. *Adding Criteria of Faith.* Christians judge all scripture, tradition, experience, and reason by Christ, who is the basic criterion of the Christian faith. Christ is known in the things that he said, the stories about his life, death, and resurrection, and in the experience of him in the lives of Christians. While that is quite easily said, and most Christians will agree, it is far more difficult to work out as we try to grow into the maturity of Christ Jesus.

But engagement with some material is never enough. Any Christian group has to struggle with the meaning and significance of these data for the individual Christian life. Here we usually have the thought of a biblical scholar, as found in the lesson quarterly, but we also have the "knowledge of Christ" in the lives of the teacher and participants. These criteria both supplement and, at times, stand in opposition to each other, but it would be a mistake to value one totally over the other. Both are needed and important.

IV. *The Process.* Every class and every teacher has a process.

The usual processes of lecture and discussion are dealt with in the next two sections, but we will look at process in general here.

I have heard teachers say, "I don't pay any attention to method or process. I just let the class do what comes naturally." In a real sense this usually means the teacher has turned the class over to the three or four talkers who will always take over and dominate what is said and done.

In recent years I have come to believe that *minimum attention to process may exercise maximum control of thought*, while maximum control of process *can* exercise minimum control over persons' conclusions. Let me give one example in the selection of reading on a particular subject. If the leader says, "Read anything you want about the meaning of the resurrection," most persons will read the things that undergird their present point of view. But, if the teacher carefully picks out in advance *several different* points of view and chooses to use a *process* that forces the participants to hear each, the exposure allows choice not otherwise available.

Process, from the arrangement of chairs to the length of the lecture, is very important.

Again, the adult is in charge of his or her own learning. The teacher or the leader, is in charge of the process of teaching. It is hoped the two will overlap, but they are never identical.

15.
Myth
Lectures are manipulative and poor teaching methods.

Reality
Lectures, when well done, can both inform and bring the insights and reflections of a trusted

leader. Since no verbal response is required, a person may disagree in his or her own mind without having to argue. Lectures are really very democratic—they allow some to doze or sleep while others plan for tomorrow.

Lectures are often interspersed with, or followed by, some form of discussion or question-and-answer period.

Go Ahead and Lecture—With a Clear Conscience

For the last thirty years, *lecture* has been a dirty word in adult education in general, and Christian education in particular. Two dozen books could be cited in which teachers are urged to forego lecturing at all, or never do it if any other alternative is available. All these books make a false supposition. "If only one person is talking, then only one person is thinking seriously, and what thinking anyone in the group is doing is being thoroughly conditioned by the lecturer." *Such an idea is not based on observable reality or experience and should be flatly rejected!*

Much of the above error is based on a further false assumption, explored in detail in the previous section, which tries to tie teaching too close to learning. Teaching and learning are, in fact, two very different processes, for which we all should be grateful. Who wants a teacher to be in charge of his/her learning?

In many ways, the *least* manipulative and coercive teaching method is a *lecture*. In fact, when considered in terms of what a lecture does *to* people, it may be the most Christian method of teaching there is! While listening to a lecture, a participant may daydream or listen very intently. The listener is free to accept, modify, or reject the ideas of the lecturer without the strain or embarrassment of trying to explain why. The listener has time to mull over a particular thought in his/her own mind while the speaker goes on to other ideas. During a lecture, the participant may be emotionally and mentally involved at a very high level, or may be struck by one idea which he or she "takes off with" and runs far afield from the subject at hand.

Thus, far from the lecturer being autocratic and arbitrary and in charge of the learning situation, the opposite condition prevails. The listener is totally free to do with the lecturer's thoughts whatever he or she wishes, and the lecturer can do nothing about it at all. At least not unless a written test is to follow—quite unlikely in an adult Sunday school class.

When I go to a lecture, or sit back to listen to a sermon, I try to have a pen and pad of paper at hand. I am not planning to take notes on the presentation; I am instead planning to listen for an idea on which I can "go to work" in my own mind. When, and if, such an idea appears, I give a silent shout of joy and begin to think furiously as its dimensions unfold in my mind and on my pad. I may hear very little more what the lecturer says, but I am really learning and am very satisfied. (My wife is often embarrassed and tries to act as if we don't belong together!)

What Is a Lecture?

A lecture is usually thought to be an orderly presentation of material by one person who is knowledgeable about, or has studied, the subject. A lecture is commonly thought to be rather formal, but most such presentations in adult Sunday school classes are not very formal and might better be described as "informal presentations," and in many cases an *interrupted informal presentation*.

What does such a presentation do? Most writers on teaching methods describe the primary value of a lecture as providing a body of information in a relatively brief period of time. While this is true of most such presentations, by far the most valuable portions of the lecture for me are the lecturer's personal reflections on the material and the lecturer's insight on the subject which the data itself does not open for me. *In brief, one of the major values of a lecture is the lecturer.* The lecturer becomes a lens through which we view a subject, and although there is always bias and distortion in what we see, there is also clarity and interest which brings the subject to life.

Thus, a well-organized lecture can present material in an orderly and logical fashion, but the lecture gains its power through the ways the lecturer views the key facets of the material and holds up to our attention the things that he or she considers to be of primary importance, or value. In fact, the *selection* of what material to include is one of the major contributions of the lecturer. The participants may have read the same material in advance (or have heard of it previously), and while listening to the lecture may say to themselves, "I never thought of that when I read it—isn't that interesting!" Furthermore, in addition to increased insight, a lecture allows the speaker to show his or her emotional reactions and commitments to certain ideas and, thus, possibly persuade the listeners to share those feelings or attitudes.

How to Give a Good Lecture or "Thirty Minutes Is Enough If—"

1. *Select* and *focus* on a few ideas—do not try to cover all the material in the lesson. You want to get the class *mentally involved in the lesson,* not hurriedly rushed over a multitude of ideas and facts. Two or three points are enough, as are only a few verses of scripture.

2. Seek for *clarity in your outline,* allowing the sequence of your ideas to be apparent to the listeners. The old saying, Tell what you are going to say, say it, and tell what you have said, is quite in order.

3. Look for and use a new twist, or a "fishhook" in the material which will catch attention and "grab" the participants' attention. You may want to give a commonplace thought "a slight turn" to make it more interesting. Develop *relevant illustrations* which tie into the daily life and experiences of the class.

4. Speak in an informal "dialogical-monologue" in which

you converse with real needs and interests, even though no one is responding out loud. You may want to ask rhetorical questions in which you also supply the answer, but during which the participants think about the response they would give if called upon.

5. Use the authorities quoted in the lesson material, but do not hesitate to do your own thinking, as well, expressing your own personality. Your personal faith and your integrity should be apparent to all. Get involved with the material and show it. Of course, be careful to clearly distinguish between your opinions and the thoughts of the authors of the material.

6. *Stop on time*—whether you are through or not! Summarize and *affirm* the key ideas.

7. Finally, to go back to the very beginning, be prepared and have something to say. No one wants to listen to an unprepared speaker.

And Then—Some Discussion

In my survey of over two thousand adult classes in four hundred churches, the use of *lecture and discussion* is increasingly preferred in adult classes.

What does it take to do it well?

1. *Adequate time.* Often a fifteen-minute lecture—presenting clearly *one* idea, followed by twenty to thirty minutes of discussion is ideal.

2. Knowing your class and depending on its size, ask "starting" questions, focused on a response to your key ideas, or simply "open the floor."

3. Control the talkers by direct and frank "look-them-in-the-eye," and say with a smile, "Joe, we've heard enough from you for awhile, let others speak now."

4. When comments come up which are "way off the subject," listen carefully to see if the speaker is trying to deal with important problems which have a connection with the lesson. If so, help the class see the relevance and

deal with it. If not, steer the group back in the direction of the lesson itself. Remember, everyone is there with burdens, pains, and questions of which most of us are unaware.

5. Note all the suggestions concerning conducting discussions in the following section.

16.
Myth
Group discussion is always better than a lecture.

Reality
While some group discussions can be very stimulating, other class discussions utilize little information and consume a lot of time in opinion swapping. Discussion can also become very manipulative as it tries strongly to persuade divergent points of view to agree with the majority. Some types of personality flourish on discussion, other, quieter persons do not.

Discussion: The Class Talking

As lectures have been disdained in adult education literature, so discussion has been honored. Thus, both good methods of teaching/learning have been overcriticized, or overpraised, and, therefore, undervalued.

Discussion can and does achieve many goals in an adult class, but it is a method which also has problems and which many consider only "a waste of time." Nevertheless, two-thirds of all adult classes have some form of discussion.

Discussion is used in adult classes in three principal ways:

1. As the *primary* method of the class in which the lesson is discussed with, or without, a designated leader.
2. Following a lecture, or other form of presentation of the lesson. Here the discussion takes off from the presentation and involves the class in exploring the lesson's implications.
3. Interspersed between short presentations, or lectures, discussing the material introduced up to that point.

When Discussion Is the *Primary* Method

1. The class must have an average attendance of no more than twenty, preferably ten to fifteen. This is essential if any major portion of the group is to have the time to express its point of view. Talking takes time, and the larger the group the more time consumed.
2. The class must have a high commitment to the idea of discussion. (If only three or four are really enthusiastic about discussion, attendance will sag or the class will die.)
3. *Several* class members must be willing to be the discussion leader at one time or another and to be prepared both to start and guide the discussion.
4. In most discussion classes there is a balance between talking about the content of the lesson and the personal agenda, or needs, of individuals within the group. If the group, or the leader, presses too hard to keep the discussion on the lesson, one of the major values of group discussion will be missed. As an example, a member of a discussion class whose child has recently died, should be able to express his/her pain, and even anger, in the midst of a lesson which does not even bear on that subject, and the class should be able both to listen to the words and the deep feelings of the person and to respond with care and insight.

    At the same time, both the class and the leader should

guard against one of the members becoming overexposed emotionally. A person can begin to shed his emotional clothes, and the class can forget that this is *not* a counseling group. It is easy for the class and leader to get "over their heads," and relationships can be permanently damaged.

5. The class needs to develop a high element of acceptance of differences without pressure either to "give in" or to force a person to agree with the majority. In *You Can't Be Human Alone* Margaret Kuhn said, "Opposing opinions are assets" in a discussion group.

6. The class should be willing over the years to study and improve its group skills. Time should be "taken out" from studying a lesson to study discussion techniques, roles, and dynamics of groups.

7. Finally, if group discussion is to succeed and not be a waste of time, every participant must take responsibility for the success of the discussion, whether he/she is the designated leader or not. (See suggested helpful books in bibliography.)

Getting the "Lesson" Before the Group

A good discussion in an adult Sunday school class is based in large part on how well the material in the lesson (including the scripture) is put before the class. This can be done in any one of several ways:

1. The leader asks each class member to read aloud, in turn, one or more paragraphs of the material.

   While this method is probably the most widely used, I believe it has great shortcomings. Persons who cannot read well are often embarrassed, as are those whose eyesight is weakening. The very time consumed and the unevenness of the reading also detract from the lesson. I would urge you to reconsider its use, because I believe it keeps many persons away, even though they rarely will say so.

2. All the class members read the lesson at home before they

come. Increasingly this rarely is done by classes, and when it is, only a few in the class have *actually* done it.

3. The lesson is briefly presented by a teacher or leader, or on occasion, the lesson is presented on audio tape, film, or closed circuit TV. This method usually works well.

4. The leader asks all class members to read portions of the lesson material *silently* for four to five minutes at a time. To do this successfully the quarterlies need to be kept in the classroom, and the class must not be asked to read very long at one time. This is actually a very good method and one which I highly recommend.

Things Group Discussion Does Well

1. Helps to digest material heard, or seen in a presentation by a process of group review, individual sharing of understanding, and enlargement of understanding through hearing the point of view of others.

2. Allows participants to verbally relate ideas heard, or read, to their own experiences and points of view, while also hearing from other members of the group in the same way.

3. Encourages participants to grow in their knowledge of one another through the interchange of ideas, feelings, and attitudes.

4. Enables participants, who wish, to express their feelings about the world around them, and possibly about one another. Other group members are, of course, free to respond to those feelings with their own.

5. Encourages participants to bring to the group their understanding of material they have read (as in a quarterly or a Bible commentary). This broadens the available information for the group.

6. Allows participants to reveal serious doubts or questions concerning the Christian faith, which they would hesitate to do under other circumstances.

Problems with Group Discussion

1. Difficulty getting it started, or getting it stopped.
2. Refusal of some to participate verbally. Some love it and thrive on it, others do not.
3. Some persons talking far too much and monopolizing the discussion.
4. Lack of material on which to base the discussion, except the previously held opinions of the participants.
5. Difficulty controlling certain persons who specialize in turning the discussion into areas quite apart from the subject—often the same by-pass Sunday after Sunday.
6. Group pressure on members to agree with the "correct" point of view. This is often done subtly by frequent attempts to say, "I believe we *really* see it the same way—possibly a *little bit differently.*"

   Even groups who pride themselves on "never agreeing" have unconscious ways of pressing for agreement by overemphasis on similarities and under-emphasizing interesting differences and the reasons for the differences.

   Much of the tendency to agree is tied to a strong desire not to get angry at one another "over unimportant details."

Participation Does Not Automatically Mean Involvement

Mr. Brown frequently asks questions and offers opinions and ideas during class discussion. He can always be counted on to participate. Sally Jones rarely says a thing in class and even when asked directly for her views she usually shies away from expressing a firm opinion. In most circles, Brown is a good participant and Jones is a poor one. Brown is considered to be more involved and is, therefore, learning more, while Jones is thought to be less involved and, therefore, learning less.

In actual fact, the exact reverse may be true. I would even

venture to say is often true. Brown's comments are usually shallow, repeated opinions long held with little careful reflection so that often they shut out new information. Brown's very participation often means that he is so busy responding that he is doing little thinking at all and is hardly involved with the ideas.

On the other hand, Mrs. Jones may be quietly listening to the new ideas, reexamining her previously held opinion to see how it fits with the new information, and is well along in the process of new clarity and new commitment. She works slowly and silently, and other persons, including her teacher, are unaware of her progress. She feels no compulsion to express her ideas, and the fact that they are as yet not thought out makes her reluctant to do so. She is, in fact, far more involved with the lesson than is the much-talking Brown and will in the end be far more affected by the session.

The teacher, in fact, has no way at all of knowing whether this is true or not. Every adult is in charge of his/her own learning!

How to Lead a Good Discussion

1. *Be realistic about time.* "We have five minutes left to discuss the lesson. Who wants to begin?" really means, "We do not have time for a discussion; so keep quiet and we will have five minutes left over!" If there are ten to fifteen minutes, the class can very well review the key ideas (in groups of three or four) and remind one another of what they have heard, but a group of ten cannot be allowed to explore their feelings about a controversial issue.
2. *Subdivide your class for discussion.* Be aware of the size of the group. Many think a class of twenty is a small group, but it is a very large group for discussion. Four to eight persons make good groups for discussion, and larger classes usually subdivide into this size group for a portion of the discussion.
3. *Relax with those who rarely speak.* You are more uncomfortable than they are. *Do not* force them to speak.

99

4. *Clarify your discussion goals.* What do you really want to happen?
5. *Listen for the values behind the words.* Often these bring persons together.
6. *Turn personal feelings toward one another back toward ideas.* Shut off old personal antagonisms.
7. *Affirm differences—even call attention to them.* Seek an understanding of the background of those differences.
8. *Withhold your own opinions until other opinions have been expressed.* Participants do not have to disagree with the leader to have a divergent idea.
9. *Work on your listening skills.* Frequently repeat what persons have said to see if they believe you have heard them accurately. Withhold judgment while ideas are being expressed.
10. *Encourage genuine expression of any idea.* Strongly discourage attempts to make participants conform.
11. *Develop the skills of summarizing.* End with a summary of key ideas and then give *your own affirmation* and summary.

17.
Myth
Adults study the Bible in their classes.

Reality
Little serious Bible study is done in many adult classes, even though they may be called adult Bible classes. Often the teacher is the only person who really studies the Bible. In too many instances what Bible study there is is about the text rather than of the text itself.

A balance of objective (from outside) and subjective (from inside) Bible study is badly needed in adult classes.

Many adults are going to Bible study groups elsewhere in order to be involved in serious study.

The Bible—Not Seriously Studied by Most

Most adult Sunday school classes have considered Bible study to be at the heart of what they do. But, recent visits to adult classes at Baptist, Disciples, United Methodist, Presbyterian, and even Pentecostal churches have shown that in *many* instances *only the teacher* ever really studies the Bible itself, even though it is carried to and from class by many participants.

I believe that more serious Bible study in adult Sunday school classes is a key to their success in the years ahead. I say often that I have rarely met a Christian adult who did not *want to want to* study the Bible. But most Christians rarely do much Bible study, even if they attend an adult class regularly.

The Bible—The Great Divider

The Bible has both bound Christians together and torn them apart. This is one reason the Bible is treated the way it is in many adult classes. The class members are afraid their fellowship will be destroyed if they get too involved in serious Bible study. Unfortunately, we can point to many instances in the past where that has exactly happened.

Adults are also well aware of persons who specialize in memorizing scripture passages and who then use that knowledge like a club to try to beat their family and friends into submission to their ideas. Such "proof-texting" has been used since biblical times to attempt to prove that one Christian is right and another is wrong. When this takes place in an adult class, it is usually quite destructive.

101

Nevertheless, most Christian adults believe that they should study the Bible and that if they do, it will strengthen their Christian life.

I have led Bible study for laypeople for many years in local churches—classes from an average attendance of three to an attendance of sixty-five. In those years I have developed some very clear-cut principles which I believe every adult class that wants to take the Bible seriously must observe.

Principles for Adult Class Bible Study

1. The Word of God is Jesus Christ, and the words of the Bible tell us about that Word. Therefore, when we study the words of the Bible we always look behind, in and through, those words for God's Word—Jesus Christ.

2. No Christian has a monopoly on understanding either God's Word or the words of the scripture. This includes biblical scholars and the most unlearned Christian peasant. Each of us must listen to one another as we seek to understand the richness of God's gifts.

3. We must assume Christian integrity in one another and not accuse one another (no matter how unusual our opinions) of being unchristian.

4. We must further assume that we will arrive at a different understanding of portions of scripture and that that will not disturb God as much as it will some of us.

5. Few of us will know Hebrew or Greek, and we, therefore, need to use a variety of English versions to try to understand the text itself.

6. While we accept differences between us, we do not feel that those differences are unimportant, nor that they should be ignored or treated as if they did not matter.

7. Different biblical understandings can remain between us and we can still be warm Christian friends. In fact, as we grow to better understand our differences, we can grow in our appreciation of one another.

The Bible in the Class

Some denominations stress that all persons bring their Bibles every Sunday, but other churches do not stress this, and most persons in those denominations do not do so. If not, *adult classes need to buy an adequate supply of Bibles and keep them in the classroom* for use each week.

If the class does a good deal of oral reading as a group, all the Bibles need to be the same translation, otherwise they could represent a variety of translations and paraphrases. A sampling of Bible commentaries, a Bible dictionary, a Bible atlas, and a Bible concordance will also be useful in the classroom. Why not build a special shelf for them?

The Risk of Being "Wrong"

An outstanding biblical scholar and teacher has said, "The key to Bible study is in running the risk of being wrong." He, like I, is concerned that adults find the desire and motivation to "get into the Bible" so that it may come alive in their lives. What he means by his statement is that we must help adults find ways to experience the biblical stories and to get in touch with the central biblical message without the fear of not being exactly correct in the eyes of biblical scholars.

All Bible study is essentially a rhythm between objective study and subjective study—between standing outside the Bible and asking as carefully as possible, historical/critical questions with as much accuracy as possible. In turn, it is important to go inside the story, try to *feel* a part of the action, and attempt to bring the impact of the biblical truth to bear upon present lives. To ask, "What does this passage say to me?" (subjective) is as important in the adult class as to ask, "What do scholars believe the author meant by this story and why is it included in this book?" (objective).

The use of both of these approaches often motivates persons to get into the Bible and to "make it their own," but the exclusive use of either approach can either become boring or

103

unchecked sentimentality. As we look at Bible study methods, it is most important to ask, "Which of these methods will interest adults in more Bible study?"

Bible Study in a Lecture Class

When lecturing, it is quite tempting to very quickly mention a large number of biblical passages which are familiar to the teacher, but are essentially unfamiliar to the listeners. If you want the class to really study the Bible during your lecture, *focus* on a *few* passages, ask everyone to read them silently, or out loud in unison, and then go back to them several times so the participants can think about each passage in a variety of ways.

Most adult Sunday school lesson material includes far more information than can be used helpfully in a class period, and in most cases, it is intended that the teacher *select* only a portion for use.

It will often be useful to have someone read the scripture passage from two or three different free-ranging paraphrases, such as Phillips or Clarence Jordan. Of course, many teachers will do this themselves as part of their lecture.

If you do not wish discussion during your lecture, you will want to engage in a "monologue-dialogue" in which you converse with the biblical story yourself in the presence of the class. Thus, you may address Paul and say, "Did you *really* mean that, Paul?" and reply back for Paul, "Yes, but I was expecting Christ to return in a very few months."

You may, of course, also use rhetorical questions when you look at the class and ask, "What kind of thoughts does that arouse in your mind?" and answer your own question by saying, "I'll bet some of you wondered the same thing that entered my mind, which was ———."

It is quite possible for a class with Bibles in hand, with thought-provoking questions to ponder, and with time allowed, to go back over the scripture passages several times in a variety of ways, *to study the Bible seriously without saying a word.*

If you want to combine a lecture with a discussion for Bible study, you will want to consider the suggestions in the next few paragraphs.

Bible Study in a Discussion Class

Of course, the comments and suggestions concerning discussion in the previous section also apply here.

It should be stressed that you may prefer to do much of your work in groups of three or four, or even in pairs at times. A good discussion is often fed by small groups first and the entire class later.

Bible study in a discussion class is quite likely to be enhanced by asking individuals to do some thinking, and possibly writing, about the passage before they start their discussion. The individual work allows persons to "get into" the passage on their own before their thinking is "taken over" by an aggressive talker.

Whether you start your work and discussion with objective questions or subjective questions will depend on your experience, but be sure to take time for both.

A variety of questions are widely used.

1. What did it say *then*?
2. What does it say *now*?
3. Now, what does it say?

. . . .

1. What is the author saying?
2. What did it likely mean to its first hearers?
3. What does it mean today?
4. If you took it seriously, what would you do?

. . . .

1. What does the passage say about God?
2. What does the passage say about men and women?

3. What does the passage say about the relationship between God and us?

· ·

1. What new idea did you have as your read the passage?
2. What puzzled you in the passage?
3. What background information would you like to know about the passage?

Many discussion leaders find it most helpful to have the class "work their way into a passage or two," first using questions like these. Then they turn to the information in the lesson material and add it to the discussion. With both the personal involvement and the data from the lesson, the following general discussion is enriched, as well as motivated.

Most good discussion leaders want to be sure the discussion does not end "just up in the air," but they try to summarize and give a positive affirmation of what has been covered.

Spectrum Bible Study

Some adult classes find it helpful to consider portions of the Bible on a spectrum from liberal to conservative. In this method the group asks, "What is the most liberal position which Christians hold on this passage of scripture?" (such as Jonah and the whale), and, "What is the most conservative position which other Christians believe?" Then other options in between are considered.

When that has been done, discuss these questions or others:
1. What is this point of view saying?
2. What values is this position trying to uphold?
3. What are some problems with this point of view?
4. What are some implications of this position?

Some persons in your class will be ready to say, "Well, once I believed that, but now I think I'm right about here, because ————." Other class members will want to reserve judgment and consider the options.

Such a method can be very educational, but it can also be extremely upsetting to those who want a more definite answer.

IV.
Myths and Realities
Concerning Curriculum

18.
Myth
Adults should learn the content of the lessons.

Reality
No one learns the content of most lessons sufficiently to recall much of it a short time later. This is even true in college where there are much higher motivations than in Sunday school.

Nevertheless, the content of the lesson, although not learned, is not unimportant. It provides the context and catalyst for learning, as well as images *and* hooks *from the material itself. These are key things the curriculum resources* actually *do.*

Teachers should make the content of the lesson transparent enough to allow the class to learn through it.

What Curriculum Resources Do Not Do

Neither the participants, the teacher, nor the writer of curriculum resources learn precisely all the details of any Sunday's lesson. Nevertheless, the investment of time and work means that the writer usually remembers more than the teacher, and the teacher remembers more than the class member. The intensity of our motivation and the extent of our work determine to a large degree how much we retain over a period of time.

There have been many surveys across our nation, trying to determine how much the typical church member knows about the Bible. Usually they reveal that few persons can name the four Gospels, that most cannot list five of the Ten Commandments, or that hardly any know the names of the twelve apostles. This often causes a great shaking of heads and a feeling among Christian educators that those who go to Sunday school aren't "learning anything!" Both the surveys and the typical reactions infer that such knowledge of biblical detail is quite important for the Christian life, and that the purpose of Sunday school lessons is to insure that the participants learn such things. Is that, in fact, what happens?

Of course, the answer is no. I have attended Sunday school most of my life (fourteen years perfect attendance as a child), and yet my knowledge or memory of the actual content of those many hundreds of lessons is very small. Does that mean the curriculum was inadequate, or the teachers were poor, or that I was simply a bad pupil? While any one, or more, of those factors may be true, that is far from the crux of the matter.

The facts are that I, as well as multitudes of others, have grown in the Christian faith over those years, have been prompted to reach out in additional directions for clarity and strength, and have felt that I have "learned Christ" in the process. While I would fail most tests on the details of the lesson's content, I am becoming a more mature Christian and I am confident the many Sunday school lessons make a real contribution to my life. What then, does the adult learn on Sunday morning, if not the content of the lesson?

What Curriculum Resources Actually Do

Curriculum resources (the plan and sequence of lessons and the materials for teacher and participant) *actually* do at least four things, in addition to conveying a vague memory of the content of the lesson.

1. The content of the lesson provides a *context* for learning and interaction.

2. The content creates a stimulus, or *catalyst*, that triggers additional thoughts and feelings.

3. The content creates *images* (mental pictures) which stick in the mind and form impressions for years.

4. The content contains *hooks* which grab the imagination and memory, and which stay with us and reappear long after the lesson is forgotten.

Let us look at each of these in more detail.

1. The content of the lesson each Sunday provides a *context*, or "arena," in which we meet one another in a new way. When Paul is our subject and we are studying his attempts to understand the relationship between men and women, the men and women in the adult class meet each other in a new context. Sally and Joe meet, not only as old friends, but also as men and women—with Paul between them and with God's spirit pulling them together. What happens? Stimulated by Paul's statements and conditioned by their experiences and feelings, pain, puzzlement, and some new understandings emerge.

A week after the lesson if Sally and Joe were tested on the exact words Paul used, or even on the problem in the early church he was trying to address, both Sally and Joe would have missed, or forgotten, many important facts. Nevertheless, both of them would consider the encounter of the lesson very worthwhile and would tell you some of their feelings, ideas, and attitudes which had been modified by taking part in *that* lesson.

Each week, the lesson provides a new *context* in which we meet again.

2. The content of the lesson provides a *catalyst* which starts the minds of some adults on new paths. Often, as I sit in an adult class, either lecture or discussion, within the first five minutes of the hour an idea is mentioned by someone which starts a new train of thought for me, often far afield from the subject of the lesson. As I fish for my pen and a scrap of paper, my mind is developing this new idea, and I am hardly listening to the lesson anymore at all. In fact, I may never get back to the lesson again! Nevertheless, if you ask me what I learned that Sunday morning, I will excitedly tell you about the stimulus of the lesson for me. I missed many details of the lesson, but did I learn!

3. The lesson content usually contains *images* which stick in the mind. An image is a mental picture, broader than an idea, because it carries with it feelings, as well as thoughts. All of us have images of the police, a politician, or Moses. Each of our images comes from experiences and information which we have accumulated over the years.

As we move into a typical Sunday school lesson, our images are often modified, or we get a new image altogether. The usual image of Job is a very patient man, but careful study reveals real puzzlement, anger at God, and impatience. Such an image is likely to stick in the mind long after the details of the lesson are forgotten.

4. The lesson often has a *hook* hidden in a very common-place paragraph, which will "reach out and grab" several persons in the class. Sometimes we are aware of the hook

during the class session, but at other times it doesn't "grab us" until several days later when we happen to be thinking in a way that opens the mind to that interesting way of thinking.

Good adult teachers are always looking for an idea which will hook the class, and they often slightly twist a trite statement to make it a more interesting "grabber."

Adults *do not* learn the details of the lesson each Sunday and remember them. But, they can get a great deal from each lesson through *context, catalyst, images,* and *hooks.*

19.
Myth
Most adults want to choose their curriculum.

Reality

Most adults are not interested in choosing their own curriculum. They prefer to leave that to someone they trust—either the teacher or a small curriculum committee. Some young adult groups, however, take great interest in what they are to study and spend a considerable amount of time making those choices. Nevertheless, these adults are a small minority.

Involvement in the choice of materials and its motivation to get one to study harder, or learn more, is essentially not true in Sunday school.

Who Wants to Choose?

Many adult educators in recent years say that adults learn best when they have an active part in designing their own curriculum or course of study. This position is based upon a variety of research, which largely focuses on self-initiated learning projects in which adults are *highly motivated* to solve a problem or achieve a personal goal. These individuals, who may be building a sailboat, or learning to use their new microwave, have a high personal stake in achieving their goals.

I am persuaded that some types of personality *will* want, and be able, to organize the reading, listening, talking, and experimenting needed to personally organize such learning, especially in consultation with a knowledgeable person. Nevertheless, there are many other persons who prefer to attend a well-organized set of lectures, with an expert-prepared curriculum on the same subjects. *With high motivation,* I am sure they learn fully as well as the other group, usually in a much shorter time.

Such experience from adult education in general, nevertheless, has little real relevance to adult Sunday school classes.

While adults want "to grow spiritually" and want "to know more about the Bible," they are rarely *highly motivated* at the moment in the same sense they are in solving an immediate personal need. The motivation is more diffuse and is rarely a feeling that a problem will be *solved* with certainty.

In Sunday school it is also true that time is quite short, and it takes a considerable amount of time to construct one's plan of learning, or curriculum.

Most denominations have two, or more, approved curriculum choices for adults. Nevertheless, from 50 to 80 percent of all adult classes use some form of the Uniform Lesson Series (also called the International Lesson Series).

Many adult classes prefer to "just use the Bible," but what that means, of course, is that the teacher and the participants use the Bible with their own background of biblical understanding, without either the enrichment or challenge, of a Sunday school lesson prepared by their denomination.

Many times I have wished my own denomination would declare such study of the Bible as "approved," but there is a fear of what will happen if adequate guidance is not provided.

In point of fact, adults want reassurance that they are not going to waste their time—that something significant is going to be dealt with, and that someone whom they find especially interesting, or whom they feel is especially well prepared, is going to lead, and has chosen the topics to be studied.

There are *a few* groups of young adults in the church who pride themselves on independent thinking and leading their own discussions and who want to choose carefully the topics they study and the resources to be used. Such groups are often made up of persons who see themselves as more liberal, or open to new ideas in religion, than most of the other adults in the church (sometimes they think their frank discussions would even "shock the minister"), and "total openness" is a symbol of their Christian stance. While every large church needs one or more such groups, experience has shown that these classes tend to get so enthusiastic about a particular idea that they "burn themselves out" and fade away after a few years.

Choice of the way in which a topic is presented, and by whom, is usually far more important than whether it is a piece of church history or a survey of a contemporary problem. Let a masterful professor of church history begin to tell and reflect on ancient incidents in the lives of long-forgotten saints, and adults are entranced and enlightened and rush to come back for more. Do they participate? Do they "learn"? Try it and see.

Criteria for Choosing Adult Curriculum

If your class wants to choose curriculum resources, where do you look and how do you choose?

1. *Start with your own denominational material.*

While there are few *major* differences in much of the available curriculum, it is true that the material produced or endorsed by your own denomination will have some points of view which are directly supportive of your own doctrine and beliefs. Check with your pastor.

2. *Include your teacher, or teachers, in the choice.*

There is nothing more negative or disheartening than to have a teacher say, "Now I didn't have any hand in choosing this material, and I don't much like it, but since we have it I'll make the best of it." *A teacher's enthusiasm for and commitment to the material being used is very important.*

3. *Consider the needs and interests of the members of your class.*

It is rarely helpful to ask the class at large, "What do you want to study?" because they do not know the options and their off-the-cuff opinions will often contradict one another. On the other hand, to offer the class a choice between specifics such as, "Would you rather study 'The Moral Teachings of Paul' or 'Help for Family Life in the Bible'?" is often motivating and helpful. Of course, you need to be sure you have a person who is interested in leading such a course. If your regular teachers do not want to, you need to look for a special teacher just for that unit.

4. *Consider the portions of the Bible and other courses you have studied in the last few years.*

Every class needs the stimulus and challenge of a varied curriculum. Ask yourselves what has been missing from your full consideration of the Christian faith.

5. *Ask how much it costs. Is it worth the difference?*

The least expensive curriculum resource is certainly not automatically the best, but cost *is* a real consideration. Stewardship of our contributions to the church should include our purchase of materials. One of the major factors to be decided in ordering curriculum resources is how many, if any, of the pupil's quarterlies should be ordered? Are they *really* used? If so, by how many? Thousands of Sunday school quarterlies are carried home at the beginning of a quarter and are thrown away unused at the end of it. Few persons receive much from them by a process of osmosis!

6. *Check the pupil's materials to see if they are written so they may be used in class.*

    An increasing number of teachers are not passing out the quarterlies and urging participants to take them home, but are rather *collecting* the quarterlies at the end of the class and giving them to each person as they arrive the following Sunday. Then, *selected* paragraphs and scripture passages are read by the class *in silence* and discussed. This gives everyone a common experience. Curriculum resources are best for this purpose if ideas are clearly divided by paragraphs and if quotations by various scholars, or authorities, are clearly identified and usable by themselves for discussion.

    Curriculum resources which are worth writing and worth buying are certainly worth using.

V.
Another Myth and Reality

20.
Myth
Adult classes do best
when the minister leaves them alone.

Reality
There has been tension between ministers and adult classes since such classes began in the early 1800s. Laypersons have resented ministers who tried to take over their class, and ministers have worried about the theology of the lay teachers and their inordinate influence over the members of their classes.

Nevertheless, there is ample evidence that the

vigor of the adult classes depends in large part on the support and interest of the minister. Most adult classes want the minister to teach them on occasion, and many teachers of adults welcome the minister's offer of training in the areas he/she knows best—Bible and theology.

Pastor's Support Should Enhance the Classes

The pastor has a large stake in the strength and vitality of the adult Sunday school classes. Such groups can either give the pastor and the church's program strong support (often being the very backbone of what is done), or they can undermine the program by direct attack or slight support.

In many churches nearly all programs of evangelism, finances, enlistment of workers, and aspects of missions and service function through the adult classes. Some pastors have tried to do away with this pattern, feeling it put too much control in the hands of class leaders. It is usually far preferable to trust, enable, and use these classes, because they represent the real capacity to get things done, and they are eager to be of help in the total life of the church.

Nevertheless, in most churches, the pastor *is* responsible for the total educational program, and at times feels required to help force classes to change policy or leadership.

One midwestern pastor tells of the teacher of a men's class who consistently opposed *every* program of the pastor and church, including telling half-truths and quite a different story to his class and the pastor. Finally, the pastor, several members of the class, and key church officials forced the removal of this teacher by merging that class with another adult class. While this is drastic action, and should be undertaken only after careful consideration, it, too, can enhance both the ultimate life of the class and the life of the church. In this case, the persistence of the minister in being "pastor" to the man over a period of years, including a long illness and finally death, repaired the break in the relationship.

117

On occasion, adult classes will import a nonchurch member with a theological point of view at *great* variance with that of the church, or the class will begin to use curriculum resources of a similar vein. Most denominations have an official policy concerning this, and it should, of course, be carried out. No adult class should be allowed to work at total cross purposes with the church, or the denomination. Members of such groups should be encouraged to change churches, so that they can worship and serve God in *basic* harmony with the host institution.

While lay officials usually handle most of the policy enforcement, the support and possible participation of the pastor is usually required.

It should be assumed that in many, if not most, churches the theology preached from the pulpit and that taught in adult classes is different. In fact, if a pastor wants to know how well his theological and biblical preaching is "getting through," he should "hide behind the door" of several adult classes and listen to the lessons when the teachers do not know he/she is listening!

The difference is, in part, between lay and professional, as it would be in any profession. It is the same difference as that between a doctor and a patient—they may both have the same fundamental understanding, but one is professionally trained and one is not. In many ways the basic difference between the clergyperson and a layperson is a theological education and an assigned responsibility by the church. I have always felt that sharing my theological education with the congregation is one of the major gifts I have to give them.

The adult Sunday school class should be a symbol of trust between the layperson and the minister. There should be no need to spy on each other or an attempt made to try to insure that the faithful teacher is conforming exactly to the minister's line.

The pastor brings his/her point of view from the pulpit, in classes taught during the week, and in daily pastoral interchange with the members. The written curriculum resources reflect the denomination's stance, and are usually close to that of the pastor.

The lay teacher modifies, ignores, questions, affirms, and

118

follows that portion of the clergy's input that seems to make sense to him/her. Nevertheless, the lay teacher is also listening to Oral Roberts, his children who are in Campus Crusade, and the skepticism of the people with whom he/she works. He is trying to survive in his marriage, be adequate with his children, and make economic, social, and political decisions which make reasonable sense to him. The lay teacher *welcomes* the minister's guidance and follows it at a distance in his own way.

Support Does Not Require Presence

Many surveys have revealed that *ministerial support is essential* for nearly everything in a church, and the adult Sunday school classes are no exception. But, some pastors say, "I have two, or more, churches, and I am always at one when the other is having Sunday school. I can *never* attend any of the classes. How can I give them much support?"

Fortunately, it is not necessary to attend, or teach, any classes to give enthusiastic support. It *is* important to believe in the values of the adult classes, to urge their support from the pulpit and in the church paper, to meet, when possible, with the teachers and the education committee, and to thank and give recognition regularly to the teachers and their work.

Support of adult classes also comes through the pastor's help in securing teachers of adult classes and in helping those teachers become familiar with the material and other teaching aids. Often the minister is the only person who has found out that a new member is an experienced teacher of adults, and it is the minister who can suggest that person be contacted by a class in need. The minister's relationship with new members also allows him/her to be sensitive to the need for new adult classes in a way that is difficult for other church leaders. This is especially true in a large church.

When Teaching a Class

Increasingly, when the pastor is free to do so, he/she is teaching adult classes on an occasional, or regular, basis. In two of the largest churches in the Southwest, *all* the ministers teach an adult class every Sunday; several of them are regular teachers of particular classes. In a few denominations, the pastor's class, often meeting in the sanctuary, has an attendance of several hundred and plays a large part in the teaching ministry of that church.

Many ministers say that they help organize new classes by teaching them themselves for the first several months. This seems to be a very fine way of adult class support.

An interesting variation is being tried by the four ministers of the Canterbury United Methodist Church, in Birmingham, Alabama. Each minister has selected several topics that he/she would like to teach to adult classes, such as, "The Gospel of Luke," or "Basic Christian Beliefs," and they have circulated the combined lists among all the adult classes, in case a class wants to sign up one of them for a period of weeks.

Support Adult Classes Through Training

Teachers often say that the biggest reward they get is when they feel they have done a good job. To do good work, they know they need as much knowledge and training as is possible, and the minister's knowledge of the Bible, Christian history and thought are very important.

The minister often offers short courses on the entire sweep of the Bible, on individual books, or on sections of the Bible. One of the things in which the minister has been trained is in the use of Bible helps: concordance, atlas, commentary, dictionary. Teachers of adult classes are supported when they also have been led in developing skills in the use of these Bible resources.

Of course, the minister always wants to be sure that the various aspects of adult education he/she offers to the congregation supports and parallels the work of the adult Sunday school classes and is not competitive with them.

Conclusion

As the reader has seen, this book advocates and urges churches to:

1. View adult Sunday school classes as a varied mixture of fellowship, learning, service, and worship which fulfill vital needs for many adults in the church.

2. See the need *both* for ongoing classes in which members stay for many years—largely based on age or marital status—and short-term, subject-centered classes with a wide age range and an emphasis on study.

3. Understand that *all* ongoing adult classes will eventually grow old and die and that *new* classes of young marrieds and young singles must be organized every few years.

4. Understand that there are few, if any, prospects for the existing adult classes in the present church membership. The prospects for these classes are newcomers to the community who are like the persons in those classes, plus the friends, relatives, neighbors, fellow workers of the present members of those classes.

5. Understand that the best way to enlist present church members in adult classes is to start new classes for them, often in combination with newcomers who have not joined a class.

6. Start new classes for particular age groups or marital status after establishing a solid prospect list, enlisting a few of them for sure, securing a good teacher for six months, choosing a curriculum unit, calling all the prospects and sending them a letter, and having a "kick-off" social event, if possible, at the parsonage.

7. Understand that many churches do not have enough prospects for a young singles' adult class and should not try, but instead should organize another middle-age couples' class or a new class for couples over seventy. *The only major way to increase adult Sunday school attendance is to start new classes.*

8. Understand that small churches (under two hundred members) usually benefit by having at least two adult classes (one of them for persons under thirty). This is the only good way to attract the young marrieds in your community. Possibly the younger class will have to meet at a time other than on Sunday morning.

9. Remember classes which seem to be growing too large do not need to be divided to maintain their enthusiasm and fellowship. They need good organization, an attractive teacher or teachers, a large enough room, and teaching methods suitable to the group.

10. Become aware of the fact that increasingly classes are needed for young singles (under thirty), older singles (sometimes for single parents), young marrieds, middle-age marrieds, older marrieds and widows (sometimes for married agains), as well as classes which are still needed for men and women only.

In larger churches, classes for any age adult—"across the board class," intergenerational groups for short periods of time, and several classes focused on a particular teaching method (serious and hard-hitting discussion) or a particular subject are needed.

Adults need to feel that a group "fits them" as well as that they fit into the group. They may say, "We are a group of questioners who probe everything," or, "We are a group who want above all else to know the Bible well."

11. Recognize that adult classes tend to focus on unique and particular enthusiasms or points of view (we are more conservative than "they are") and these enthusiasms tend to produce *energy* for the church. (They say with pride, "We always buy the Bibles for the children!") As long as these classes do not become exclusive and divisive and see themselves as a unit in the whole church, they are essentially positive. Attention must always be given to seeing the classes and the entire church program as a whole.

12. Realize that much-important fellowship and informal learning goes on around the coffeepot and at class social events. Both are important.

13. Remember that adults can be motivated to teach and to take training if they are recruited for realistic periods of time, and if training is focused and is of high quality.

14. Value adult teachers who are very well liked—"nearly worshiped"—and are usually valuable S. R. O.'s.

15. Provide a more mature, possible role model, as a teacher for young adults. They want to be involved in discussion of the lesson, but they rarely want to teach themselves.

16. Remember that adults are in charge of their own learning, and no matter what is taught or how it is taught they will exercise their *bunk* detectors and screen what they find to be valid or true. They may do most of this silently.

17. Understand that both lecturing and group discussion have their limits and values and are largely a matter of taste and preference in adult teaching/learning.

18. Encourage adult classes to study the Bible more seriously than at present by combining objective and subjective approaches.

19. Recognize the fact that adults are at many different points in their spiritual and intellectual lives, and they should be encouraged and enabled to study on the level they desire. Those who always want to chew tough meat are not more Christian than those who want to continue to drink the milk of the faith.

20. Remember that "knowing" and "doing" are quite different things, and most adult classes neglect mastering the "skills" of implementing the faith.

21. Understand that the content of each Sunday's lesson will not be learned and remembered by most adults, but the content *will* supply a context, a catalyst, images, and hooks from which the adults will learn and remember.

22. Train teachers to utilize the lesson materials. Since most adult class members do not study their lessons at home, curriculum materials can be prepared for use *in* class during the lesson.

23. Ask the teacher or a small curriculum committee to select lesson materials. Few adults want to choose their own and would rather someone they trust choose for them.

24. Accept the fact that some adults do not want to join an adult class ever but prefer to get their Christian education individually and through the worship services. *They also are learning the faith.*

25. Understand that the pastor of the church is always the key person in the life of the adult classes. If the pastor supports the classes from the pulpit, shows interest in them, and sometimes teaches them, they will usually prosper. If not, they will nearly always decline.

Suggestions for Using This Book

The myths in this book are intended to call to your attention many of the major issues and problems in adult Sunday school classes. Some of the myths and realities will be far more important for your church than others.

It is suggested that the list of myths and realities be used to *survey* the program of adult Sunday school classes by clergy, professional Christian educators, or lay workers with adults. Some churches will wish to organize a small study group for this purpose. It may be a group with official responsibility, such as a committee on education or an adult council, or it may be a special group set up just for this purpose.

You will, of course, find some realities with which you disagree strongly, saying to yourself, "That certainly is not true in our church!" Both the myths and realities are generalizations which point to *a* truth but hide, or ignore, other truths. In our several denominations and the many different regions of the country we have many differences.

At other points, the truth of the reality will confirm what you already knew or suspected. You will then possibly ask, "What can be done?" The paragraphs in each section of this book may give some suggestions, or the books in the bibliography may be of help.

There are some hard realities in this book which many adult classes find difficult to accept. Nevertheless, it is quite important that the findings of your committee be shared with adult class officers and teachers as widely as possible.

Bibliography

Anderson, Philip. *Church Meetings That Matter*. Philadelphia: United Church Press, 1965.

Kuhn, Margaret E. *You Can't Be Human Alone*. New York: Association Press, 1956.

Little, Sara. *Learning Together in the Christian Fellowship*. Atlanta, Ga.: John Knox Press, 1956.

Schaller, Lyle E. *Assimilating New Members*. Nashville: Abingdon, 1978.

Adult Development References

Erikson, Erik. *Childhood and Society*. 2d ed. New York: W. W. Norton & Co., 1964.

Levinson, Daniel J. *The Seasons of a Man's Life*. New York: Alfred A. Knopf, 1978.

Lowenthal, Marjorie Fiske, et al. *Four Stages of Life*. San Francisco: Jossey-Bass Inc., 1975.

McGill, Michael E. *The Forty to Sixty-Year-Old Male*. New York: Simon & Schuster, 1980.

Sheehy, Gail. *Passages, Predictable Crises of Adult Life*. New York: E. P. Dutton, 1974.

Faith Development References

Fowler, James, and Keen, Sam. *Life-Maps: Conversations on the Journey of Faith*. Needham Heights, Ma.: Wexford, 1977.

Whitehead, Evelyn Eaton, and Whitehead, James D. *Christian Life Patterns*. Garden City, N.Y.: Doubleday & Co., 1979.

Wilcox, Mary M. *Developmental Journey*. Nashville: Abingdon, 1979.

Single Adult References

Brown, Raymond Kay. *Reachout to Singles*. Philadelphia: The Westminster Press, 1979.
　　Centering on singles on the West Coast, this book helps the reader understand singles and gives many suggestions for largely non-Sunday school programming.

Dow, Robert A. *Ministry with Single Adults*. Valley Forge, Pa.: Judson Press, 1977.
　　Stresses the *pastoral* aspects of ministry with singles. Surveys the life-styles of single adults, and has some suggestions for programming.

Hensley, J. Clark. *Coping with Being Single Again*. Nashville: Broadman Press, 1978.
　　Deals with the issues from a rather conservative, but open, standpoint.

Lawson, Linda, ed. *Working with Single Adults in Sunday* ͢ Nashville: Convention Press, 1978.

LeFeber, Larry A. *Building a Young Adult Ministry*. Va͡ Judson Press, 1980.
　　Stresses an innovative, largely non-Sunda͡ young adults. Centers on experiences in ͡ New York.

Wood, Britton. *Single Adults Want to Be the Church, Too.* Nashville: Broadman Press, 1977.

A very helpful, comprehensive book, written by the former minister to singles, Park Cities Baptist Church, Dallas.

Older Adult References

Burns, Robert J. *A Program for Older Adults in the Church.* Grand Rapids: Baker Book House, 1976.

Clingan, Donald F. *Aging Persons in the Community of Faith.* Christian Board of Publication, P. O. Box 179, St. Louis, Missouri 63166, 95 cents.

A *very* comprehensive booklet on the subject.

Hessel, Dieter, ed. *Maggie Kuhn on Aging.* Philadelphia: The Westminster Press, 1977.